A Feast for Lent

Keep the word of God, for 'blessed are they who keep it'. Let it pierce deep into your inmost soul and penetrate your feelings and actions. Eat well and your soul will delight and grow. Do not forget to eat your bread or your heart will wither, but let your soul feast richly. If you keep the word of God in this way without a doubt you will be kept by it.

St Bernard of Clairvaux (1090–1153)

The Bible Reading Fellowship

BRF encourages regular, informed Bible-reading as a means of renewal in the churches.
BRF publishes three series of regular Bible reading notes: *New Daylight*, *Guidelines* and *First Light*.
BRF publishes a wide range of materials for individual and group study. These include resources for Advent, Lent , Confirmation and the Decade of Evangelism.
BRF publishes introductory booklets on Bible-reading, group study guides, training aids, audio-visual material, etc.
Write or call now for a full list of publications:

The Bible Reading Fellowship
Peter's Way
Sandy Lane West
Oxford
OX4 5HG
Tel: 0865 748227

A Feast for Lent

Delia Smith

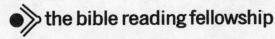 the bible reading fellowship

The Bible Reading Fellowship
Peter's Way
Sandy Lane West
Oxford
OX4 5HG

First published 1983
Reprinted 1983, 1984, 1985, 1986, 1987
New edition 1992
Reprinted 1993

The scripture quotations are from:
The Jerusalem Bible © Darton, Longman & Todd Ltd and
Doubleday and Company Inc. 1966, 1967 and 1968
The Revised Standard Version © Division of Christian Education of
the National Council of the Churches of Christ in the United States
of America 1952, 1957 and 1971
The Psalms: a new translation © 1963 The Grail (England)

Cover illustration: F. N. Colwell

British Library CIP data applied for

Printed and bound by Cox & Wyman Ltd, Reading

*For Frances Hogan who taught me
how to see, hear and understand God
in scripture.*

Grateful thanks to my husband Michael, who edited and typed the manuscript, and guided me throughout. Thanks also to Fr James Walsh OSB, the Sisters of Jesus and Mary, and all the members of my own parish in Stowmarket. It is in this community that I have been formed as a Christian, and I thank them for their encouragement, support and prayers.

Except for the Psalms, almost all the scripture quotations are from the Jerusalem Bible as used in church books. The Psalms are from the Grail version. The verse references are those in the Bible, whilst the numbering of the Psalms in the Grail version is given by the figures in square brackets.

Contents

Foreword

Delia Smith needs no introduction. Her television series in the kitchen has pulled aside the veil of mystery that (for the uninitiated) surrounds a steaming steak and kidney pie or a rich rice pudding. She has opened many eyes to see how simple it can be to produce food that is good to eat. I know of several priests who (in these days when the ministry of housekeeper seems to be in decline) maintain that Delia Smith should occupy one of the major teaching posts for training of future priests.

I am glad that she has produced this book of her own reflections on the biblical passages associated with Lent. She may be able to do for the scriptures what she has done for the kitchen. Many people for whom the Bible is a mysterious and uncomfortable book will be encouraged by her meditations and perhaps helped by them to read the Word of God for themselves.

Delia Smith is writing about her own voyage of discovery. Her choice of readings (and the sharing of her thoughts and prayers as she reads) takes us through the steps of conversion—that change of heart and mind that must begin with the recognition of our own weakness and reach out for peace in the compassion and kindness of God.

This is a helpful and hopeful book, where the Word of God steps out of the past to become a personal and moving experience in everyday life. It is an experience we could all come to share more deeply this Lent.

Victor Guazzelli, Auxiliary Bishop of Westminster

Introduction

By way of introduction to this new edition of *A Feast for Lent* perhaps I can share a little of the history of how this book came into existence exactly ten years ago.

What, you might well wonder, would a cookery writer be doing writing a book of scripture meditations? Well, the series of events that led up to it began in 1981 with a phone call from a BBC producer who was making a series called 'Home on Sunday'. Would I take part? I agreed, and one sunny day that summer Sue McGregor and a delightful film crew came to my home and made a 40-minute film about me and my faith.

After the programme had been transmitted I received a letter from the Bible Reading Fellowship asking me to share some of my personal reflections on scripture in a book for Lent. Now I happen to believe that absolutely anyone who ponders quietly and reflects on a passage of scripture will always be given fresh insights, and that it can act as a sort of spiritual springboard encouraging the deep and more reflective part of our nature to surface.

In agreeing to undertake the task I understood that my own notes would be entirely personal; others would discover many other meanings to those same passages. Scripture, like art, needs nothing from our side other than sitting before it, looking, listening and giving it time to do what it will. Quiet reflection is *not* study, and the two should not be confused. Some days there will be a barren, empty table, and on others there will be a rich feast we can hardly tear ourselves away from.

Perhaps I can end this introduction with one of the great promises of scripture which says: 'If you make my word your home, you will indeed be my disciples. You will learn the truth and the truth will make you free' (John 8:31-32).

Delia Smith
Lent 1992

The Appeal

'Come back to me with all your heart, fasting, weeping, mourning.'

Let your *hearts* be broken, not your garments torn. Turn to the Lord your God *again*, for he is all tenderness and compassion, slow to anger, rich in graciousness, and ready to relent.

(Joel 2:12–13)

Ash Wednesday begins with an appeal from the very heart of God himself. The appeal is a familiar one: it echoes through the whole of scripture. In the Old Testament, the Gospels and New Testament what we hear over and over again is God calling his people to himself, inviting them into a relationship with him—a relationship that promises renewal, healing, a fullness of life, in fact a share in the life of God himself.

Ash Wednesday is a time for the drifting, wandering people of God to turn back, to re-commit themselves to this relationship in a deeper way ('Come back to me with *all* your heart'). It's a time to take stock. How much of my heart is 'turned to God'? Is it just a small percentage, for a short time on Sunday, a few minutes night and morning or when everything else is done?

Today we must 'let our hearts be broken not our garments torn'. Originally the tearing of garments was an outward

15

sign of repentance, but in the 'eighties I suppose giving up smoking or chocolate would be the equivalent. But God asks more. What he's most interested in (and it mentions this twice) is the heart. Our self-denial will be meaningless if we don't allow God to touch our hearts during these forty days of preparation.

This almighty God who created heaven and earth, who is so high above us that we can barely begin to grasp who he is, promises that every wound, every fault, every sin will be dealt with with tenderness and compassion.

Today we would do well just to meditate on this inspiring description of what our God is like, not forgetting that he is also 'rich in graciousness'. In Isaiah (30:18) we read that 'God is waiting to be gracious'. If we allow ourselves to enter into this deeper relationship to which he calls us, we will soon begin to understand this wonderful graciousness.

While, inevitably, there is much that is not in harmony with him, he doesn't come crashing in making great demands we cannot cope with. No, he comes to absolve us, rescue us and to save us with perfect and sensitive timing that is appropriate for each and every individual. In this relationship—as in any other—we will experience joy and sorrow, freedom and discipline, but God will always be gracious, never asking more that we can give (yet in his wisdom always knowing what that is).

Today we can parallel our forty days ahead with the story of the Exodus, in which we are gradually being rescued from the darkness of our lives (Egypt) and prepared in the wilderness for Easter and the resurrection (the Promised Land). Of course what we will note in this comparison is that it took the Israelites forty *years* of mistakes!

We have much to learn, naturally, and he has more and more to teach us. Our struggles and trials are the same as the Israelites. Listen to how God describes the reasons for what was happening to them during that time: 'To humble you, to test you and to know your inmost heart' (Deuteronomy 8:12). And a few verses on: 'God was training you as a man trains his child' (v.5).

Today then, let us begin a new journey, a journey into a closer relationship with God. Let our mourning and weeping be that of regret for the times we have not allowed God to touch our inmost heart—and pray that during the next forty days he will do just that.

Prayer
> *Father, I thank you that you are*
> *all tenderness and compassion,*
> *slow to anger and rich in graciousness.*
> *Help me to receive this truth*
> *in my inmost heart, so that*
> *it will free me and rescue me from the fear*
> *and anxiety and all that keeps me*
> *from you. I ask you this*
> *through Jesus Christ your son*
> *who lives and reigns with you and*
> *the Holy Spirit, God for ever and ever.*
> *Amen*

Meditation Read Psalm 51 [50]

Choose—life or death   *Thursday*

'I set before you life or death . . . Choose life, then, so that you and your descendants may live, in the love of the Lord your God, obeying his voice, clinging to him; for in this your life consists.'

(Deuteronomy 30:19–20)

Today's reading is a tiny clip from a very beautiful passage that needs to be read in full. It's all about making a decision—a decision to choose God. In the life of Moses we see a foreshadowing of the life and role of Jesus. Moses is God's representative, who mediates, who passes on the

17

word of God to the people. Just before his death he summarizes the whole of God's programme for the people (the Covenant). The essence of the text is this: it doesn't matter how far you have wandered from the truth, however far away you are, 'the Lord your God will gather you and have pity on you once again'. If the people return to the Lord (i.e. repent), his compassion will always await them. But they must return fully, in wholehearted commitment ('With all your heart and soul' v. 2).

The message concerning this decision is a strong one. Those who choose not to return to the Lord are heading for disaster: those who choose to turn their backs on God and worship false gods and idols (in today's terms such gods are wealth, power, position, self-seeking pride, etc.), they are set on a course for death. Those who emphatically and deliberately choose to turn their backs on God and his blessings are turning their backs, in fact, on life. They may return to God at any time, but if they choose not to, they then choose death.

But what of those who do choose life? Perhaps a whole-hearted commitment seems a little daunting, but further on in the text God promises all kinds of help. Choosing life is merely the first step: in verse 6 there is a truly wonderful promise as to what will then happen: 'And the Lord your God will circumcise your heart ... until you love the Lord your God with all your heart and all your soul, and so *have life*'.

In other words what he is saying is this: choosing life is just a start. After that the Lord promises to bring about certain changes. People who have wandered far away will find their hearts hardened by their stubbornness. In the Acts of the Apostles, when Peter first preached after Pentecost, the people were 'cut to the heart'. What God promises here in verse 6 is to 'circumcise your hearts'. He takes on the responsibility of changing and softening their hearts, so that they will be submissive and eventually be able to love him and have life. (For the Jews physical circumcision was an outward symbol of the Covenant; in addressing the Jews here God is saying, 'It's the inward sign I'm looking for'.)

But that's not all. In verse 8 we find another promise. Something else is going to happen, something *very important*: 'and once again you will obey the *voice* of the Lord your God'. Put in even simpler language, what this is saying is once your heart is restored, your hearing will improve! Here we find a truth that really needs to be reflected on. Those who are far away from God have great difficulty hearing him! Jesus underlines this point in John: 'He who is of God *hears* the words of God; the reason why you [the Jews] do not hear them is because you are not of God' (John 8:47 RSV).

The next promise in the Deuteronomy text is very reassuring. Those who choose life, who choose to be obedient, are not choosing something beyond their capabilities. 'This law that I enjoin on you today is not beyond your strength nor beyond your reach' (v.11). Then in verse 14, 'No, the word is very near to you, it is in your mouth and in your heart'. God's programme then is this: return to me, allow me to change your heart, so that you can hear my word (i.e. scripture), and receive and obey it. And *if* my word is on your lips and in your heart, all this is not going to be beyond your grasp.

Prayer
> *Your word is a lamp for my steps*
> *and a light for my path.*
> *I have sworn and have determined*
> *to obey your decrees.*
> *Lord, I am deeply afflicted*
> *by your word. Give me* life.
> *Accept, Lord, the homage of my lips*
> *and teach me your decrees.*
> *Amen*
> (Psalm 119 [118] : 105–107)

Meditation Read Deuteronomy 29

What sort of fast? *Friday*

Fasting like yours today will never make your voice heard on high. Is that the sort of fast that pleases me, a truly penitential day for men? Hanging your head like a reed, lying down on sackcloth and ashes? Is that what you call fasting, a day acceptable to the Lord? Is not *this* the sort of fast that pleases me ... to break unjust fetters and undo the thongs of the yoke, to let the oppressed go free, and break every yoke, to share your bread with the hungry, and shelter the homeless poor...?

(Isaiah 58:4–7)

Although Lent has always been associated with 'fasting' and penance (self-denial), the tradition goes back a lot further than Lent. Centuries before the birth of Christ, God, through the prophet Isaiah, was warning people in no uncertain terms about the wrong kind of fasting!

But before we look at the problem, let's first examine what lies behind the tradition. It seems that originally fasting was something that accompanied mourning as a sign of sorrow; then later it began to accompany prayers of petition as a sign of sincerity, or to be used as a sign of religious preparation— as we see in the lives of great holy men like Moses and Daniel, and of course in our Lord's own forty days' fast in the wilderness as a preparation for his ministry.

Fasting, then, was an outward sign, an expression of something that was happening inside a person. What happened in Isaiah's time was the perennial problem of religious hypocrisy: even though the people's hearts were far from God and his laws (they were unjust, disobedient, neither generous nor loving to others), they nevertheless kept up an outward show of being religious—something that is abhorrent to God. In the time of Jesus the Pharisees were masters of deception in this area. Our Lord vividly describes the problem when he says in Matthew 23 that they are like 'white-washed tombs' that look good on the outside, but inside are full of 'every kind of corruption' (23:27).

For us as we get deeper into this season of penance, we need to take a close look inside ourselves—for me personally always a daunting prospect! But what I've discovered is what we discussed on Ash Wednesday, that 'God is waiting to be gracious'. The first thing we have to grasp is that self-denial is not a display of human muscle-power: 'Look, I've given up smoking—I've been through this terrible agony for God' or 'I'm going to force myself to be nice to that horrible so-and-so whatever the cost'.

In chapter 58 of Isaiah we find a beautiful description of what exactly should be happening. Note the word yoke is mentioned three times, as in 'untie the thongs of the yoke'. What this means is, break free from all that enslaves you and allow others to break free as well. God is not demanding a great show of human effort as proof of our love. What he wants is for us to be free from all that enslaves us. Suppose I am a very jealous sort of person and this causes pain, not only to me but to all those who are close to me. God is not saying I've got to overcome that jealousy or else! He says, 'Don't be a slave to it. Let's look at and begin to undo all the causes, so that you can be free.' In Genesis 1 God's message to mankind is 'Go, fill the earth and conquer it. Be masters of it.' We are to be masters of our lives, enjoying freedom not slavery.

To sum up. Let us approach our Lenten acts of self-denial with the right sort of attitude, an attitude which will allow the Lord into some of our problem areas, to rescue us and save us. As we prepare to celebrate the Lord's triumph over sin and death in the Resurrection, let us understand that this can happen in each and every one of our lives, whoever we are, whatever kinds of problems we have.

Let's end with what Jesus said: 'I tell you most solemnly, everyone who commits sin is a slave. Now the slave's place in the house is not assured, but the son's place is assured. So if the Son *makes* you free, you will be free indeed' (John 8:34–35).

Prayer from a Psalm
> *O search me, God, and know my heart.*
> *O test me and know my thoughts.*
> *See that I follow not the wrong path*
> *and lead me in the path of life eternal.*

(Psalm 139 [138] : 23–24)

Darkness into light   *Saturday*

> If you do away with the yoke, the clenched fist, the
> wicked word, if you give your bread to the hungry, and
> relief to the oppressed, your light will rise in the
> darkness, and your shadows become like noon. The
> Lord will always guide you, giving you relief in desert
> places.
>
> *(Isaiah 58:9–11)*

Today's reading is a continuation of yesterday's. The
culmination of chapter 58 of Isaiah is a very great
promise: for those who *are* willing to do away with the
yoke (that is, to be rescued from all that binds and enslaves
them), who *are* willing to turn back to God and allow him to
rescue them from their anger (the clenched fist and wicked
words), for them something will begin to happen in their
lives. A light will rise in the darkness.

Scripture is filled with images like this—the word is
reflected in nature and nature reflects back the word. God
communicates through his creation, using words and
pictures so simply and directly that sometimes we almost
miss the point.

When we examine this image of a light in darkness, we can
picture that moment in nature when dawn begins to break
through, a blackened sky with a faint light in the distance
suddenly beginning to spread, first of all creating an eerie
half-light producing shadows, then breaking out into a

radiant and dominating light that banishes all shadows and darkness and makes everything visible.

The message of Isaiah 58 is a simple one. Whatever our problems, whatever yoke we're tied to (jealousy, greed, bad temper, stubbornness—the list is endless, but basically it's whatever is outside our control), if we submit these problems to God's intervention, gradually the whole situation can be illuminated and changed. And if we're in any doubt, God's promise is quite definite: 'the Lord your God will *always* guide you' and 'give you relief in desert places'. He will give us relief in those difficult areas as we journey through the wilderness of our lives. We may well feel nothing much is happening spiritually, but every now and then we will receive the reassurance that he is still leading and guiding us.

If we are going to take Lent seriously, today we need to spend some quiet peaceful time just asking the Lord to show us any dark areas in our lives that are outside our control, and then praying that he will shed more of his light on them. Let us remember, too, that the greatest part of what God was promising through the prophet Isaiah was not that we should save ourselves, but that he was sending us a saviour. It's in the life of Jesus that we can find encouragement and help in our own struggles.

Chapter 3 of St John's gospel has much to say about light and darkness and new beginnings. Jesus says: 'God sent his Son into the world, not to condemn the world but so that through him the world might be saved ... Though the light has come into the world men have shown they prefer darkness to the light because their deeds were evil ... but the man who lives by the truth comes out into the light, so that it may be plainly seen that what he does is done in God' (John 3:17–21).

Prayer

> *Shed your bright light, O Lord, upon our lives and from your children of light banish the deeds of darkness.*

23

Return

Then Jesus was led by the Spirit out into the wilderness
to be tempted by the devil. He fasted for forty days and
forty nights, after which he was very hungry, and the
tempter came and said to him, 'If you are the Son of
God, tell these stones to turn into loaves'. But he
replied, 'Scripture says, "Man does not live on bread
alone but on every word that comes from the mouth
of God".'

(Matthew 4:1–4)

Ever since the third chapter of Genesis the Bible has been
the continuing story of man's repeated failure to overcome
the powers of evil. The people are unfaithful to the covenant
(the marriage contract), they fail to respond to God, to love,
trust or obey him.

In today's passage Jesus begins his public ministry. In
order to grasp his role in our destiny, I think it's important
to appreciate that he was truly human as well as divine. This
is best understood if we reflect on his ordinariness. Born and
reared in humble surroundings (Nazareth was considered
to be the back of beyond—see John 1:46), and now aged
about thirty, he is about to embark on his public life. But
first he is led by God into the wilderness to confront the
enemy of man *as man*. True, divine power was always at his
fingertips—he could command twelve legions of angels to

25

his side if he so wished (Matthew 26:53)—but that wasn't the answer.

In the Garden of Eden it seemed that Satan had overcome human nature, but God's ultimate plan provided for that. In the words of St Leo the Great, 'When the designated time had come, which God in his deep and impenetrable plan had fixed upon, God's Son took the nature of man upon himself in order to reconcile man to his creator. Thus would the devil, the father of death, be himself overcome by that self-same human nature which he had overcome.'

This divine plan is foreshadowed in the Old Testament. God leads his people into the wilderness to test them, train them and teach them—and they continually fail. Jesus is also led into the wilderness, but he does *not* fail, even though in his hunger he is offered the entire world. Thus the human weakness of the first Adam is overcome by the new Adam, before he has even begun to preach.

The forty days in the wilderness was a time of preparation leading up to the greatest event in history. As we commemorate the same forty days of Lent, we too need to prepare for the celebration of Easter, when mankind was eternally reconciled to God. We can learn a great deal from the whole of the above text (i.e. verses 1–11). Jesus always answers the tempter with scripture, emphasizing that we must live 'on every word that comes from the mouth of God'. Scripture is the word of God and it is that which feeds our faith. Three times Jesus says 'It is written' when he gives his replies. Satan, too, uses a scripture passage to try to catch him out, but Jesus (the man) has been feeding on the word of God all his life and is able to answer with equal knowledge and conviction. For us, preparing for Easter, it is vital to feed daily on the word of God too.

Prayer
> *Lord, as I read and reflect on your holy word today, open my ears to hear you and my heart to receive you.*

Meditation Read Deuteronomy 8

Are you dissatisfied?   *Lent 1 / Monday*

> Oh, come to the water all you who are thirsty;
> though you have no money, come!
> Buy corn without money, and eat, and at no cost
> wine and milk.
> Why spend money on what is not bread, your
> wages on what fails to satisfy?
> Listen, listen to me, and you will have good things to
> eat and rich food to enjoy. Pay attention, come to
> me; listen, and your soul will live.
>
> *(Isaiah 55:1–3)*

This is a call to the dissatisfied, those who are heavily burdened, weighed down perhaps with the cares and pressures of the world. So often people who labour for what the world has to offer—riches, security, success, friends—find very little satisfaction in attaining them. In every human being there's a deep-down ache that only God can satisfy. For some the ache can be dulled by extreme activity or ambition; for others the ache is recognized but not understood, kept carefully hidden behind an appearance of contentment. How often have we read about suicide cases where the relatives and friends of the person have said they behaved quite normally the day before it happened?

Every serious sin has its roots in need: the sexual pervert, the drug addict, the alcoholic, the person who commits adultery, all are crying out with a desperate need that none of these things can satisfy. A bottle of whisky may dull the ache, but when the whisky wears off the ache returns.

Today, with the build-up of nuclear weapons, falling social values, and a general atmosphere of insecurity, the ache of dissatisfaction grows more pronounced and people become more vulnerable to the influence of strange and powerful cults. On the surface these seem to offer some kind of answer, but in reality they cause havoc: young people are brainwashed, families split, idols—pictures of ordinary

27

human beings—venerated and worshipped. (We have witnessed the horrific consequences of this in our time, such as the mass-suicide of hundreds of men, women and children in South America.)

But Jesus came for sinners, and when we look at his life we see the mind and heart of the Father reflected in it. Jesus *chose* to keep company with sinners. His attitude was one of total compassion, because, unlike the self-righteous and self-satisfied Pharisees, sinners understand their need. Of all people sinners understand the incompleteness of this life.

I once heard a great preacher saying that he actually preferred preaching to hardened criminals in a prison than to Sunday morning church worshippers, because, he said, they responded so much more.

When I was a small child I could never understand what Jesus had actually saved us all from. But just as a child has to learn by experience that fire burns, so we have to experience our own poverty and weakness. We have to learn that our weakness causes us to sin, and that sin is destructive. Therefore, we need to be saved—to be rescued—from its destructive influence, to live safe and secure in God's protective love.

To the dissatisfied, to those who have an unrecognized ache within them, God says this, 'Oh, come to me! *All* who thirst and hunger shall be filled. I can provide everything. Come, pay attention, listen. I am the source of life. "Listen and your soul *will* live." '

Prayer
> *Lord, make me know your ways.*
> *Lord, teach me your paths.*
> *Make me walk in your truth, and teach me;*
> *for you are God my saviour.*
> (Psalm 25 [24] : 4–5)

Do not be afraid   *Lent 1 / Tuesday*

Do not be afraid, for I have redeemed you; I have called
you by your name, you are mine. Should you pass
through the sea, I will be with you; or through rivers,
they will not swallow you up. Should you walk through
fire, you will not be scorched and the flames will not
burn you. For I am the Lord your God, the Holy One of
Israel, your saviour . . . you are precious in my eyes . . .
you are honoured and I love you . . . Do not be afraid, for
I am with you.

(Isaiah 43:1–5)

The book of the prophet Isaiah has been described as being
amongst the greatest works of literature ever written.
Certainly it's a much quoted work, and some of the
passages are as familiar and famous as those of the gospels.
What Isaiah is prophesying is no less than the turning-point
in the history of the people of God—the coming of the age of
Immanuel (God with us), an age when all the peoples of
earth will have access to the one true God.

Someone once said that the words 'Do not be afraid'
occur 365 times in the Bible (that's once for each day of the
year!). I'm afraid I haven't checked this out, but it seems to
me that fear is something that dominates many people's
lives. It can become almost like a thick wall that separates
them from God. Behind the wall of fear they cannot see or
hear him properly—therefore they cannot perceive the only
real and sure security there is. Without God fear becomes a
snare from which there is no escape.

Earlier on in Isaiah there's a story which illustrates this
point. The people's hearts are far from God, and through all
the history of God's people in the Bible one clear pattern
emerges: when the people turn their backs on God they
always end in trouble. In this instance the trouble is that
they are about to be invaded. They are so afraid that 'the
heart of the king and the hearts of the people shuddered as

the trees of the forest shudder in front of the wind'. Isaiah is sent to the king with a message from God: 'Pay attention, keep calm, *have no fear*'. What the king has to pay attention to is that unless the people are with God, and God with them, they cannot survive. 'If you do not stand by me, you will not stand at all' (Isaiah 7:9). Here lies the answer to all fear. But it doesn't end there, because throughout the rest of Isaiah we hear that God is going to do something new. There is a bubbling excitement as the age of the Messiah is proclaimed, when all fear will be conquered. 'Strengthen all weary hands, steady all trembling knees, and say to faint hearts, "Courage! Do not be afraid. Look, your God is coming . . . he is coming to save you." Then the eyes of the blind shall be opened, the ears of the deaf unsealed, then the lame shall leap like a deer' (35:3–6).

However, returning to the passage at the beginning, this is one we need to read in a very personal way, if (as it says in John's first letter) 'In love there can be no fear, but fear is driven out by perfect love'. We all need to grasp God's love for each of us, one to one, so his love can begin to cast out fear in our lives. Many of us spend our existence longing to be loved, to be honoured, to be precious in someone's eyes. Yet all the time that is precisely how we *are* loved, by God who created each one of us, totally individual, totally unique. Each of us is very special and 'precious in his eyes'. 'I have called you *by your name*. You are mine.'

Prayer

> *So let every good man pray to you*
> *in the time of need.*
> *The floods of water may reach high*
> *but him they shall not reach.*
> *You are my hiding place, O Lord;*
> *you save me from distress.*
> *(You surround me with cries of deliverance.)*
> (Psalm 32 [31] : 6–7)

Seeing God   *Lent 1 / Wednesday*

If you will not listen, my soul will weep in secret for your
pride; my eyes will weep bitterly and run down with
tears, because the Lord's flock has been taken captive.
(Jeremiah 13:17 RSV)

I once asked an experienced spiritual director, someone who
had given retreats and directed countless souls in their
search for God, what was the main difficulty that people
encountered when they attempted to relate to God? She said
that without doubt two major blocks existed in people's
minds. One was a poor self-image, and the other a poor
God-image (we will discuss the first elsewhere in the book).

The poor God-image was a kind of unawareness, or lack
of experience, of the personal love of God. People keep God
at arm's length because of a subconscious fear of judgement
and condemnation. So while he's kept at a distance, as it
were, they never really get to experience his tenderness and
compassion which is 'rich in mercy'. It is so easy to
misunderstand God, to imagine he simply demands—
love, fidelity, obedience—and if we cannot live up to the
demand we can settle for a kind of nodding acquaintance
that doesn't get too involved.

One of the most precious ways to grasp the true image of
God is through scripture. Once again—even at the risk of
being over-simple—I would assert that when you begin to
search the scriptures it is almost like looking through a
photograph album full of images which can communicate a
person. As you delve further through the album, so the
image becomes clearer and clearer. The above passage is one
such image. Time and again we get a glimpse of how God
feels when we refuse to let him love us and provide for us.

The first such image I ever came across in the Old
Testament was when God (very early on) grew tired of
man's wickedness and, it says, 'regretted having made man
on the earth'. We don't hear of his anger; instead there are

31

three profound and telling words. 'His heart grieved' (Genesis 6:6). And that's not all, because while he had made up his mind to put an end to creation, something softened and changed that decision: Noah—'a good man' and full of 'integrity' (6:9). Though his heart grieved, God's love of man prevailed and, through Noah, humanity was given another chance. (Returning for a moment to the photo-album analogy of the Bible, it is as if many of the pictures and images in the Old Testament are prefixed with little arrows that point to Jesus. In Noah we see a type of Christ, one good man who wins salvation for the rest of the world through a new creation. After the cleansing of the flood, the waters of baptism.)

Through Jeremiah we hear again of the grief of God, only this time the picture is even more vivid. The people will not listen; their pride prevents them from hearing the word of God. They are heading towards a future of oppression and captivity. When this happens to his people God's eyes 'weep bitterly and run down with tears'.

We see this same aching compassion in Jesus himself. In Luke's moving account of his entry into Jerusalem on Palm Sunday, 'As he drew near and came in sight of the city he *shed tears over it* and said, "If you in your turn had only understood . . . the message of peace! But, alas, it is hidden from your eyes!" ' (Luke 19:41–42).

Prayer
> Lord, teach me to know you. Open my eyes to see you, to understand you and to understand your message of peace.

Seeking God   *Lent 1 / Thursday*

I know the plans I have in mind for you—it is the Lord who speaks—plans for peace, not disaster, reserving a future full of hope for you. Then when you call to me, and come to plead with me, I will listen to you. When you seek me, you shall find me, when you seek me with all your heart; I will let you find me. (It is the Lord who speaks ...)

(Jeremiah 29:11–14)

These are words from the prophet Jeremiah, one of the greatest prophets of all. His life was very close to that of Jesus himself, a life of sacrifice, torture and ridicule. It is through the books of the prophets that we hear God speaking directly to his people, and through Jeremiah in particular that we hear God lamenting the people's unfaithfulness, and warning them of the disaster they will bring on themselves. Outside God's grace the people are doomed: their false gods and idols cannot help them. In chapter 2 God's words are explicit, 'my people have exchanged their Glory for what has no power in it ... my people have committed a double crime: they have abandoned me, the fountain of living water' (2:11, 13).

In an attempt to avert the coming catastrophe God is compelled to deliver his warning through Jeremiah. The people do not heed it, are defeated by their enemies and their temple is destroyed; they are reduced to a faithful remnant. Yet while Jeremiah is the mouthpiece for God's warnings and judgement, he also at the same time describes God's tender compassion for his people—illustrated so beautifully by the passage above.

Total commitment is what the Lord is after. A flirtation, a half-and-half attitude, won't do. 'When you seek me with all your heart, I shall let you find me.' Repeatedly it's the attitude of the heart that's called into question. If we think we have to labour night and day to seek God with a mighty

33

concentration of human effort, we're wrong. All we need is a pure heartfelt desire to seek him for himself alone, and then he *lets* us find him—like a mother who plays hide-and-seek with a very small child simply to give him pleasure and deliberately allows a bit of herself to stick out of her hiding-place, so that the child will soon find her and experience joy in the search.

It's great passages from scripture like this one that underline the simplicity of God's love for his children (a love that's constantly reflected between a mother or father and a very small child). True, there has to be a certain amount of discipline, but over-riding that is always the sheer joy of the parent/child relationship.

I once watched a child of about three on a railway platform. As the train drew in her gaze fixed on the opening doors, neck straining, slightly anxious. Then came the moment of recognition and joy, then a run at full speed down the platform, and a leap up into her father's out-stretched arms. Whether he had been away for a year, a month or a day I couldn't tell, but the moment of reunion was sheer joy. What God is saying through Jeremiah is, 'I have plans for you, plans for your future. Come to me and I will listen to what you have to say. If you decide you *really* want to seek me then I promise I will *really* let you find me.'

Prayer

> *Show me, Lord, your way*
> *so that I may walk in your truth.*
> *Guide my heart to fear your name.*
> (Psalm 86 [85] : 11)

Be reconciled

And for anyone who is in Christ, there is a new creation; the old creation has gone, and now the new one is here. It is all God's work. It was God who reconciled us to himself through Christ and gave us the work of handing on this reconciliation . . . So we are ambassadors for Christ; it is as though God were appealing through us, and the appeal that we make in Christ's name is: be reconciled to God.

(2 Corinthians 5:17–20)

How I would have loved to have been present when Paul was preaching: I would have loved to have seen the look in his eyes, the expression on his face, and heard the sound of his voice! Of course 2000 years later we can still hear this greatest of all preachers through his letters. The passage of time has not in any way affected the dynamic power of his message. Even now we can experience the gut-feeling that permeates all his teaching, and we are left in no doubt that Paul was indeed an 'ambassador for Christ' and that God was, and still is, quite definitely appealing through him. Through Paul's letters we hear God appealing to us not just as a universal church but also as individuals, because in Paul we have access to a personal teacher and communicator.

It's said that personal experience authenticates preaching: it's not what you say, it's what you are. So what Paul is saying to the Corinthians is born of experience of the most extreme kind. In Paul the 'old-creation' was a vicious persecutor and killer of Christians, the 'new creation' a humble travelling evangelist who, through his message, not only inspired the early church but continues to give life to it two millennia later.

Paul explains this phenomenon in one very short sentence: 'It is all God's work'. Mere human beings do not have the power to change their lives. Only the reconciling power of God through Christ can begin the work of a new creation in a person.

Paul is appealing to the Corinthians simply to come forward and say 'Yes' to being reconciled to God. The work of reconciliation may be God's work, but the Corinthians need to consent to the work being carried out. In Lent Christians are called to do the same, to return to God and re-commit themselves to his transforming influence in their lives. Reconciliation is not a once-off happening, but a lifetime of re-creation. Anyone who *has* said 'Yes' to the transforming power of Christ can actually experience the old creation gradually passing and the new one taking its place. Isaiah's prophecy about the mission of Jesus affirmed that it will 'rebuild the ancient ruins . . . raise what has long lain waste' (Isaiah 61:4). The people of God need not fear about wasted years or ruined lives: reconciliation can restore, reform and re-create.

We'll find (along with Paul himself, quoting Isaiah in his appeal to the people) ' "At the favourable time I have listened to you; on the day of salvation I came to your help." Well, *now* is the favourable time; this is the day of salvation' (2 Corinthians 6:2).

Prayer

> *The Lord is my shepherd;*
> *there is nothing I shall want . . .*
> *Near restful waters he leads me,*
> *to revive my drooping spirit.*
> (Psalm 23 [22] : 1, 3)

Eagle's wings   *Lent 1 / Saturday*

Did you not know? Had you not heard?

The Lord is an everlasting God, he created the
boundaries of the earth. He does not grow tired or
weary, his understanding is beyond fathoming. He
gives strength to the wearied, he strengthens the
powerless.

Young men may grow tired and weary, youths may
stumble, but those who hope in the Lord renew their
strength, they put out wings like eagles.

(Isaiah 40:28–31)

If we keep God at a distance in our lives, he can seemingly
become smaller in our minds—not in stature but in
effectiveness at a personal level. We can accept that he
created heaven and earth perhaps, but thereafter he is
relegated to a kind of father-figure, a divine overseer who
watches over us but can't really effect any change in the lives
of individuals. We may love him, pay homage to him, but we
don't actually expect anything of him.

In this situation he is diminished by our lack of response,
knowledge and real perception. In the Bible those principal
characters who encountered God's greatness and magnifi-
cence at first-hand found their lives changed dramatically.
Moses when he heard the voice of the Lord at the burning
bush 'covered his face, afraid to look' (Exodus 3:6). Isaiah's
reaction was one of fear and remorse: 'What a wretched state
I am in! I am lost, for I am a man of unclean lips and I live
among a people of unclean lips' (Isaiah 6:5). Peter, when he
suddenly understood that he was standing before the
Messiah, the son of the living God, was so overcome that
he 'fell at the knees of Jesus saying, "Leave me, Lord; I am a
sinful man" ' (Luke 5:8).

Now *we* can't actually see God face to face in all his glory
until we pass from this life, but we must nonetheless draw as

near to him as possible. 'Come close to God' (it says in James 4:8) 'and he'll come close to you.' It's in this coming closer that God begins to reveal himself, and we can begin to be filled with wonder at his power and greatness. Perhaps, then, we might protest with the Psalmist, 'Too wonderful for me, this knowledge, too high, beyond my reach'! (Psalm 139 [138] : 6)

But nothing is too high or beyond our reach. As we read at the start, those who hope in the Lord *renew their strength* and they begin to fly like eagles. It is a beautiful and telling analogy. The eagle is the king of birds: if he uses the wings God gave him, learns to stretch them out to their full potential and be carried along on the air currents (the wind of the Holy Spirit), he can fly higher than any other bird, so high that none of his enemies can reach him. He is totally free.

God is calling us to renew our strength, be like eagles, totally free of our enemies (that is, anything that can prevent us realizing our full potential as a human being). Today read chapter 40 of Isaiah, in order to meditate on the greatness of God and the wonder of his promises to us.

Prayer

> *You, O Lord, are my lamp,*
> *my God who lightens my darkness.*
> *With you I can break through any barrier,*
> *with my God I can scale any wall.*
> (Psalm 18 [17] : 28–29)

Repentance and Conversion

Cleansing waters

> 'I shall pour clean water over you and you will be cleansed; I shall cleanse you of all your defilement and all your idols. I shall give you a new heart, and put a new spirit in you; I shall remove the heart of stone from your bodies and give you a heart of flesh instead. I shall put my spirit in you, and make you keep my laws and sincerely respect my observances.'
>
> *(Ezekiel 36:25–27)*

All through the Bible water symbolizes God's grace and its cleansing, saving power. Thirst, in turn, symbolizes a person's deep need for this saving power—and perhaps this is most vividly illustrated by the psalmist who cries out, 'Like the deer that yearns for running streams, so my soul is yearning for you, my God. My soul is *thirsting* for God, the God of my life' (Psalm 42 [41]:1–2).

In the natural sense water is obviously essential to life: nothing can live or grow without it. By analogy people without God become dry and parched, and will eventually die unless they come to the waters of life to be cleansed and revived. At the time of Noah it was water that cleansed the earth of defilement and, through Noah, we were given a new start. Ezekiel's prophecy here is pointing to Christ, whose spirit will powerfully change people's lives, cleansing and renewing them. And still today the purifying waters of baptism symbolize what the spirit of God will accomplish in the life of the baptized person: the work of the Holy Spirit in our lives is one of restoration, restoring us to our full and eternal potential.

Lent is a time to renew our baptism, especially its cleansing aspect. John's baptism on the banks of Jordan was a baptism of repentance to 'prepare the way of the Lord'. If we are to prepare ourselves we must be open to cleansing water. The water may be symbolic but the cleansing is real: just as we need to wash our bodies to get rid of the dust and dirt of our daily life, so spiritually the same thing needs to happen—we can become very dusty spiritually. (Apparently Lent means 'spring' in Middle English, so we might even say that Lent is the time for spring-cleaning!)

We cannot, of course, save and purify ourselves. It is, as St Paul says, 'all God's work'. It is God who says I will cleanse you, give you a new heart, and will put my spirit in you. Then the more we allow God to cleanse us, the more cleansing we'll find we need. Have you ever washed a spot off some paintwork, and then found the difference in the colour underneath meant you had to get to work on the whole lot?

But let us remember also that the positive effects of having a bath is that we emerge feeling good, restored, refreshed.

God's promise through Ezekiel that we started with today is confirmed by Jesus: 'If any man is thirsty, let him come to me! . . . From his breast shall flow fountains of living water' (John 7:37–38). The promise of God's grace, the gift of the Holy Spirit for anyone who comes, will renew the life of that person in such a way that it will flow out to others as well.

Prayer

> *Have mercy on me, God, in your kindness.*
> *In your compassion blot out my offence.*
> *O wash me more and more from my guilt*
> *and cleanse me from my sin.*
>
> *(Psalm 51 [50] : 1–2)*

Repent and be converted: conversion
Lent 2 / Monday

> For thus says the Lord your God, the Holy One of Israel:
> Your salvation lay in conversion and tranquillity, your
> strength, in complete trust; and you would have none of
> it . . .
>
> But the Lord is waiting to be gracious to you, to rise
> and take pity on you, for the Lord is a just God. Happy
> are all who hope in him.
>
> *(Isaiah 30:15, 18)*

These verses from Isaiah sum up the whole of God's
relationship with his people, both collectively and individually, throughout the whole span of history. In the first
half of chapter 30 the Lord is rebuking the people who turn
their backs in rebellion, warning them that without him they
will eventually be 'irretrievably shattered', smashed 'like an
earthenware pot'. The human race may strive and toil for
power, but all the time their only lasting strength is trust in
God.

Salvation is only possible through conversion, and conversion and repentance are one and the same—a changing of
direction, retracing our steps and returning to God. Repentance is not an overnight transformation which we bring
about ourselves. It is not a case of 'Today I'm short-
tempered, over-indulgent and self-centred but tomorrow
I'll repent and it will all have gone'. That's *not* what it's like.
People shy away from repentance precisely because they
misunderstand it. True conversion and repentance is very
simply and humbly turning back to God and saying, 'I'm
short-tempered, over-indulgent and self-centred: can you
help?'

Then there's another level of repentance which can be
rather more difficult for us (not for God), and that's when
we don't *know* what we need to repent of even though we're

41

aware we need to turn to God in deeper conversion. Here the format is still the same, still simple: 'Lord because I want to turn to you in a deeper way, *show* me my sinfulness and teach me to repent'. (This second type of repentance we will discuss more fully later in the week.)

In verse 18 we have what must be one of the most beautiful and comforting verses in the Old Testament: while we may choose to rebel against God—or indeed struggle to turn back to him—all the time God is waiting for us. And not just waiting for us to return but waiting *to be gracious* when we do, to rise and take pity on us. The love that God has for us and the extent of his forgiveness are hard for mere human beings to grasp, but if we really reflect on the meaning of this verse and take it right into the very depths of ourselves, at least we can begin to understand the immense love of the Father for his creation. This image of the Father patiently waiting to show pity is clearly echoed by Jesus in the story of the prodigal son: that is our reading for tomorrow, so let us today meditate in a very personal way on these verses which provide a context, as it were, for Jesus' parable.

Prayer

> *O send forth your light and your truth;*
> *let these be my guide.*
> *Let them bring me to your holy mountain*
> *to the place where you dwell.*
>
> *And I will come to the altar of God,*
> *the God of my joy.*
>
> (Psalm 43 [42] : 3–4)

The prodigal son   *Lent 2 / Tuesday*

> 'While he was still a long way off, his father saw him and was moved with pity. He ran to the boy, clasped him in his arms and kissed him tenderly.'
>
> *(Luke 15:20)*

In the story of the prodigal son we are shown the key that opens the door of repentance. Yesterday we read in Isaiah how the Lord would rise up and take pity on us, and here we can see it actually happening. It is a very well-known story—all the same we really need to give time to reflect on it in a prayerful way during Lent.

The first point to note in the story is that the boy *chooses* not to live in community with his father. As he is perfectly free to choose, the father can do nothing about that: once the boy has left home he is beyond the reach of his father—but by his own choice. Many people choose to go their own way in this life—and repentance (as we've said before) is turning *back* to God. Now the interesting point in verse 20 is that while he was still *a long way off* the father was moved with pity and *ran* to the boy. It is of no consequence that we might be a long way off too: if there's a change of heart the Father comes running out to meet us. Like the prodigal son, if a person has reached the very end of themselves, literally lying in the gutter of sin, one glance homeward to God, one moment of repentance, and the Father is out on the road with outstretched arms.

'He clasped him in his arms and kissed him tenderly.' If you remember the photograph album that explains the scriptures, here is a very clear snapshot of what God's love is like. The only problems are (*a*) that we can't believe it, and (*b*) that we can't accept it because we think we don't deserve it. The boy actually protests and says, 'I no longer deserve to be called your son'. The father's reaction to this is to *quickly* put a ring on his finger and the best robe on his back, and then to kill the fatted calf. No one can ever deserve God's love. 'Deserve' is a word that has no place in the spiritual life and must be eliminated from its vocabulary. In truth all we can do is *allow* God to love us.

Notice also that the father said to the servants 'Quick! bring out the best robe, ring, sandals ... ' When a sinner repents, turns back to God, he receives great blessings very quickly—and more than that (as is brought out so vividly in this story), there is the joy of it all. 'We are going to have a feast, a celebration, because this son of mine was dead and has come back to life; he was lost and is found.' Repentance is not gloom and doom, sackcloth and ashes. It is being rescued and set free, and we must learn how to celebrate being reconciled to God, how to enjoy being loved and accepted no matter how far we have strayed. As Jesus said in this same chapter (vv. 6–7), 'Rejoice with me ... I have found my sheep that was lost ... I tell you, there will be more rejoicing in heaven over one repentant sinner than over ninety-nine virtuous men who have no need of repentance'. Today, read and reflect on verses 11–24 of Luke 15; as you begin to look closely at the boy's father, so you will begin to see a vivid picture of God the Father.

Prayer

> *As a father has compassion on his sons,*
> *the Lord has pity on those who fear him;*
> *for he knows of what we are made,*
> *he remembers that we are dust.*
> (Psalm 103 [102] : 13–14)

The elder brother   *Lent 2/Wednesday*

'He was angry then and refused to go in, and his father
came out to plead with him; but he answered his father,
"Look, all these years I have slaved for you and never
once disobeyed your orders, yet you never offered me
so much as a kid for me to celebrate with my friends".'

(Luke 15:28–29)

The story of the prodigal son does not end with joyous
celebration. The father has another son, and this son we find
on closer examination has a greater and more serious
problem than the first one. If we are seeking God and
attempting to relate to him in a serious way, we will find that
both brothers have a tremendous amount to teach us.

The elder brother is suffering from the deadliest sin of all,
pride, which in his case manifests itself in anger, resentment, stubbornness and (worst of all) self-righteousness.
This story, remember, is being told to the scribes and
Pharisees who complained that Jesus was keeping company with sinners, and had actually eaten with them! In the
first half of the story Jesus deals with the sinners and their
situation: the second half is aimed directly at the Pharisees
who are accusing Jesus in just the same way as the elder son
is accusing his father.

What we see paralleled here provides us not only with the
touchstone to repentance and conversion, but also the key to
understanding the issue at stake in the Christian vocation.
We have pride versus humility. In a way it almost seems that
the sin is irrelevant: it is the *attitude* of the sinner which is
the point at issue.

The younger brother understands his own weakness and
his need to be included in his father's household even in a
very humble position of servant. Having fully understood
his weakness, what he encounters is love, peace, joy, and the
very best of everything. The elder brother in contrast is not
aware of his weakness. He thinks he has earned his father's

love: 'all these years I have slaved for you'. He is the muscular Christian, the one who goes about doing good, does everything right, obeying all the rules. But underneath he's suffering from anger, jealousy and resentment. He isn't at peace and is unable to celebrate. Neither can he love, or even say the words 'my brother'—instead he refers to him as 'this son of yours'!

All his problems *could* be dealt with. The father loves him just as much. 'My son, you are with me always and all I have is yours.' But pride rules, just as it did with the Pharisees who obeyed the law to the letter and did all the right things. Because they were unable even to consider their faults and weaknesses, the challenge of Jesus got too much for them and they had to put him to death.

In any programme of repentance it is necessary, with God's help, to examine ourselves and learn to ask for help like the younger brother, and at the same time to understand that problems once realized and accepted can be dealt with—but pride and self-righteousness (like the elder brother's) close the door on love. And a person who has closed the door on love can never be truly at peace. Let us ask the Lord for the grace to be humble, to be open to an understanding of our weakness, and to allow him to rescue and change us.

Pragyer

> *Examine me, Lord, and try me:*
> *O test my heart and my mind,*
> *for your love is before my eyes . . .*
> *(Psalm 26 [25] : 2–3)*

The stubborn heart   *Lent 2 / Thursday*

'The heart is more devious than any other thing, perverse too: who can pierce its secrets? I, the Lord, search to the heart.'

(Jeremiah 17:9–10)

A stubborn heart is weighed down with troubles, the sinner heaps sin on sin. There is no cure for the proud man's malady, since an evil growth has taken root in him.

(Ecclesiasticus 3:27–28)

True repentance can only be approached with an open mind, which is the mark of real humility—while a closed mind is the result of pride and stubbornness. The problem is well illustrated all through the gospels by the example of the scribes and Pharisees, whose minds are completely shuttered. The dishonesty of their outward show of religion lies in the fact that their hearts are far from God—and the sad thing is that they are powerless to help themselves, for as Jeremiah remarks, the heart is more devious than anything. True, God can pierce its secrets, but he cannot penetrate the heart of a stubborn person. The author of Ecclesiasticus likens this to a disease where the patients are *incapable* of hearing the word of God, even though he comes to them in the person of Jesus and speaks directly to them.

God forewarned Isaiah of this frightening condition in people, and Jesus himself reflects it in Mark's gospel: 'they may see and see again, but not perceive; may hear and hear again, but not understand; otherwise they might be converted and *be forgiven*' (Mark 4:12; 'healed' in Isaiah 6:10). The healing can only come after a humble opening-up to what God wants to accomplish in our lives. If my heart is devious, then I must allow God to pierce its secrets.

The alternative is devastating—like the course of a disease, to return to the metaphor in the second passage

47

above. A stubborn refusal to *allow* God to save us from our sinfulness is like a cancer that takes root. And as cancers grow, they are harder to get rid of and affect other parts of the body. In this case it starts, spiritually, to destroy our hearing and causes blindness, so that eventually we end up like the Pharisees who are incapable of seeing or hearing God.

We'll finish on a positive note, though, with a scene from our photo album: in this one Jesus is sitting at a table eating with tax-collectors and sinners. Notice he's not standing up on a platform preaching a sermon, or doing anything other than just being with them where they are. He is prepared to identify with them. Of course it horrifies the Pharisees, to whom it was quite unacceptable even to mix with anyone who was morally or professionally disreputable. So they ask, Why? And Jesus' answer is: 'It is not those who are well who need the doctor, but the sick. I have not come to call the virtuous, but sinners to repentance' (Luke 5:31–32). The irony in this, of course, is that the sinners in question were much closer to the kingdom of God than the Pharisees— who in their stubbornness failed to recognize their need of the doctor.

Prayer

> *Happy the man whose offence is forgiven,*
> *whose sin is remitted.*
> *O happy the man to whom the Lord*
> *imputes no guilt,*
> *in whose spirit is no guile.*
> (Psalm 32 [31] : 1–2)

An open mind   *Lent 2 / Friday*

'If only you knew what God is offering, and who it is that is saying to you "give me a drink", you would have been the one to ask, and he would have given you living water.'

(John 4:10)

In the story of the prodigal son we had examples of the two attitudes to God's love and forgiveness. Today we look at another gospel character, one who illustrates perfectly the disposition needed for a complete programme of repentance, conversion and witness to the love of God in the world: the woman at the well.

Today, before reading these notes, it's essential to read John 4:1–42. The whole story is like a drama enacted on a stage, the principal character being God (played by Jesus) and humanity (played by the Samaritan woman). The plot is of how God approaches one particularly human being, and how that human being responds. Whilst we know that Jesus is truly God, the scene opens with a reminder that he became truly man: he sends his disciples off to get some lunch and has a rest, because the journey has made him tired. He sits down by a well and while he's there a woman arrives to get some water.

She is some kind of misfit; she has a problem relating to people and this is fairly evident from the fact that she's alone and not with the rest of the women. (It was frowned upon for a woman to be out alone in the society of those times.) Unknowingly she is just the sort of person God wants to reach out to. Let's look at Jesus' approach. At other times in the gospels we see his anger and frustration with the self-righteous, but in dealing with this rather sad, broken life his approach is extremely gentle.

The first thing he does is ask her for a drink. He, who is God, who existed before the beginning of the world, humbles himself before humanity and begs a drink! Here by the well he is a human being asking for a drink: on the cross he is God crying out 'I thirst' for the whole of humanity to be reconciled. The woman's reaction is a kind of disbelief—What, you (a Jew) ask me (a Samaritan)? Many people cannot believe God wants to draw them to himself, because they simply don't feel good enough.

In Jesus' reply we can discern a kind of longing on his part: *'if only you knew what God is offering'*. For her part she desperately needs to know what God *is* offering, and who this is standing before her. At the moment she can only see at a practical human level, so she raises one or two objections. The well is deep, he doesn't appear to have a bucket . . . but she's *still interested* and goes on to ask him what kind of man he is. Is he greater than Jacob who built the well?

Now we are beginning to see precisely the quality that's needed in every human being: quite simply, an *open mind*. She hasn't dismissed his first enigmatic remark and gone on her way. She wants to hear him out. His reply is positive. 'Anyone who drinks the water that I shall give will never be thirsty again: the water that I shall give will turn into a spring inside him, welling up to eternal life.' For the woman, with her receptive mind, this is the moment of conversion—and conversion is simply asking, 'OK, I want it, please give it to me.'

After conversion the next stage is repentance. She is standing before God asking for eternal life. Again let's watch carefully how Jesus deals with repentance—none of the skills of modern psychology could have dealt with it more subtly or gently. He does not accuse or condemn, he just gently helps her to face herself. 'Go and fetch your husband.' 'I have no husband.' 'That's true, because although you've had five, the one you are living with now is not your husband.' This is exactly how repentance happens—God, gently, lovingly and with perfect timing helping us to face ourselves. Her immediate reaction to this is so typical. She changes the subject. She recognizes that he is a prophet and begins to question him about religion.

Jesus doesn't press her on her problem; instead he

explains that the hour is coming when the Holy Spirit will teach the truth. She replies that she knows that when the Messiah comes 'he will tell us everything'. She has passed all the tests of spiritual life with flying colours. She has an open mind, she's willing to listen, she's prepared to face herself. Jesus responds by revealing himself fully. '*I who am speaking to you, I am he.*'

The blessings of open-mindedness, repentance and belief inevitably flow out to others, and at the end of the story we learn that 'many Samaritans of that town had believed in him on the strength of the woman's testimony'.

Prayer
> *You do not ask for sacrifice and offerings,*
> *but an open ear.*
> *You do not ask for holocaust and victim.*
> *Instead, here am I.*
>
> (Psalm 40 [39] : 6–7)

The open door   *Lent 2 / Saturday*

'I am the one who reproves and disciplines all those he loves: so repent in real earnest. Look, I am standing at the door, knocking. If one of you hears me calling and opens the door, I will come in to share his meal, side by side with him.'

(Revelation 3:19–20)

No reflection on repentance would be complete without this famous passage from the Book of Revelation. The message is in fact a warning to the church in Laodicea which, spiritually, has grown lukewarm. The people were materially well-off but spiritually 'wretchedly and pitiably poor, blind and naked too'. They must return to God in real earnest—the warning is blunt and to the point, but as always spoken in love. 'I am the one who reproves and disciplines all those *he loves*.' To reprove is self-evidently to point out someone's faults; though in its modern sense we tend to associate the word 'discipline' with strict enforcement and regimentation, the root of the word is in *learning*—the instruction of disciples in a proper course of action. Jesus offers to teach us because he loves us and even those who are lukewarm can, if they repent, still learn.

The painting that hangs in St Paul's Cathedral called 'The Light of the World' shows Jesus holding a lantern and knocking on a door. The door has no handle. We presume the handle is on the inside, and only the person within can open it. The door must have been closed for many years as it is covered in plants and weeds. It's not a work of art to everyone's taste, but the message is beautiful and it illustrates this scripture passage perfectly: Jesus stands knocking at the threshold of our hearts all our lives. Only we can decide whether or not to open the door to him and invite him in.

What he also says is, 'If *one* of you hears me calling ...' The call is individual, one to one. And then the promise: 'I will come in to share his meal, side by side'. From earliest times the religious symbolism of sharing a meal was that it established sacred ties between those who shared it, both with each other and with God. Thus the eucharist has become central to Christian worship.

The Lord will come into our lives through an open door, teach us and share with us at a very deep level ('side by side' indicates the intimacy of this bond). If we look back to the sinners and tax collectors, we see they *had* opened the door and the Lord was prepared to share a meal with them *where they were*. Jesus comes right into the messiness of our lives. Where we are caught up in sin, where we have problems relating to people, where we are sick, anxious, depressed, afraid, lonely—those are precisely the areas he wants to enter and share side by side.

If that sounds easy, it *is*! What prevents this from

happening in a person's life is human pride, an unwilling-
ness to face the reality of our own poverty and weakness.
Blessed are the poor in spirit—blessed are those who
understand the poverty of the human condition without
God. The key to repentance, then, is first of all to realize that
human effort alone cannot achieve true repentance; then to
realize therefore our need of a saviour to free us from the
problem areas of our lives; and finally to open the door and
allow this to happen.

Prayer

> *Indeed you love truth in the heart;*
> *then in the secret of my heart teach me wisdom.*
> *O purify me, then I shall be clean;*
> *O wash me, I shall be whiter than snow.*

> (Psalm 51 [50] : 6–7)

Listening to the Word

The awakened heart

Come in; let us bow and bend low;
let us kneel before the God who made us
For he is our God and we
the people who belong to his pasture,
the flock that is led by his hand.
O that today you would listen to his voice!
'Harden not your hearts.'

(Psalm 95 [94] : 6–8)

In the collection of prayers and scripture readings that makes up the daily prayer of the church, the breviary or divine office, this psalm is recited at the beginning of each day before all the other readings. It emphasizes daily the importance of listening to the word of God—*on a daily basis*.

The psalm itself commemorates the tragedy that occurred during the Exodus, when those who rebelled against God and refused to believe that he could lead them to the promised land, were left to die in the wilderness (Numbers 14). During Lent, the time of recommitment, these words remind us that we must come into the presence of the Lord *each day*, to kneel before him and listen to his word, to allow him to be the God of our lives and lead us by the hand.

Throughout scripture, in the Hebrew tradition, the heart represents a great deal more than its purely physical function. For the Jews the heart incorporated all the things that modern man associates with the mind—memory, logic, reasoning. All through the Bible—and indeed all religious thought—the heart represents the deepest centre of the whole make-up of a person. It is in this deep centre that God communicates himself. Another psalm (42 [41]) expresses this communication as 'deep calling on deep in the roar of the waters', God manifesting himself in this spiritual heart—if we allow him to.

For those of a poetic turn of mind there is a beautiful description of how a 'heart' is gradually awakened to God in the Song of Songs. 'I sleep, but my heart is awake. I hear my Beloved knocking. "Open to me . . . my love" ' (5:2). In the midst of our daily toil, while trials and uncertainties, joys and sorrows revolve around us, deep is calling on deep, our 'hearts' are being awakened. So, do not deny this happening, do not 'harden your hearts'. Learn to listen, learn to be led out of the wilderness of your daily life and to enter into the deep peace of communion with God.

'O that today you would *listen*' means acknowledging this deep place within me, where I can begin to listen and receive the word. God will begin to speak to me about me and in due course I will understand that, whoever or wherever I am, I am part of the people who 'belong to his pasture'.

To begin this week of readings on the word, read chapter 3 of the Letter to the Hebrews, which provides a meditation on Psalm 95 [94].

Prayer

> *. . . I through the greatness of your love*
> *have access to your house.*
> *I bow down before your holy temple,*
> *filled with awe.*
>
> (Psalm 5:7)

God speaks   *Lent 3 / Monday*

Yes, as the rain and the snow come down from the
heavens and do not return without watering the earth,
making it yield and giving growth to provide seed for
the sower and bread for the eating, so the *word* that
goes from my mouth does not return to me empty,
without carrying out my will and succeeding in what it
was sent to do.

(Isaiah 55:10–11)

St John's gospel begins: In the beginning was the *word*. If
we go right back to the beginning of the Bible we
immediately hear the revealed word of God. 'God said' . . .
'God said'. Every time he spoke, something happened. God
said, 'Let there be light' and there was light. From the very
start we learn that God's word is a creative and dynamic
force in the world. The psalmist confirms, 'He spoke; and it
came to be. He commanded; it sprang into being' (Psalm
33:9).

While still in Eden Adam and Eve could hear God in the
normal physical sense—they 'heard the sound of the Lord
God walking in the garden in the cool of the day'. After the
banishment God continued to speak to man, but through an
intermediary, and the Bible is a complete record of the
spoken word. Abraham, Moses and the various prophets
who were commissioned to mediate and speak the word in
the Old Testament were often reluctant, but so powerful
was God's word within them that they were compelled to
deliver it in spite of their resistance. The word was always
inspired by God's Spirit, as indeed we affirm every time we
say the creed: 'We believe in the Holy Spirit . . . who has
spoken through the prophets'.

Collectively the prophets are like signposts along a road,
each one pointing to the greatest event in history—the word
made flesh. For three years the word of God was addressed
to the people not through patriarchs and prophets, but by

God himself. Thus we, two thousand years later, have through the written accounts of all that was said during that time direct access to all that God is wishing to say to us. 'Nothing is hidden' said Jesus 'but it must be disclosed, nothing kept secret except to be brought to light' (Mark 4:22).

Throughout all four gospel accounts we find Jesus emphasizing, re-emphasizing, literally pleading with the people to *listen* ('let anyone who has ears to hear, listen'). The word of God has the power to change people's lives utterly. As the rain waters the earth to make it yield and give it growth, so it is with us. If we listen attentively to the word of God, we will begin to yield and respond to it. We will grow spiritually and the fruits of our growth will even provide for others—'seed for the sower, bread for the eating'. Jesus himself confirms this at the end of the parable of the sower. Those, he said, who *'hear the word and accept it*, yield a harvest of thirty, sixty and a hundredfold' (Mark 4:20).

Today, meditate quietly on the parable of the sower (Mark 4:1-9) and in the light of yesterday's reflection, compare the image of the deep centre—the open heart—with that of the rich soil where the word of God takes root in preparation for a rich harvest.

Prayer
> *My soul is waiting for the Lord,*
> *I count on his word.*
> *My soul is longing for the Lord*
> *more than watchman for daybreak.*
> (Psalm 130 [129] : 5–6)

The word and the spirit   *Lent 3 / Tuesday*

'Those who do not love me, do not keep my words. And
my word is not my own: it is the word of the one who
sent me. I have said these things to you while still with
you; but the Advocate, the Holy Spirit, whom the Father
will send in my name, will teach you everything and
remind you of all I have said to you.'

(John 14:24–26)

Yesterday we reflected on the role of God's word—how it
accomplishes God's purpose in carrying out his will. Today
we can listen to Jesus himself speaking about the word, and
the essential message we are given is that everything he has
to say comes directly from God the Father, and that
everything God wants to say to us is said by Jesus. 'To
have seen me' he told Philip 'is to have seen the Father'. The
closer we come to the word of God with open ears and
hearts, the closer we come to the whole mystery of the
Trinity. Here (and in the rest of chapter 14 of John) we are
assured that, though Jesus' time on earth is at a close, the
Father will be sending the Holy Spirit to be present in the
world and in each of those who believe in his Son.

Here is the key to understanding the words of Jesus, and
indeed the whole of scripture. In simple terms, we have
been given a divine personal teacher, without whom the
books of the Bible are merely record, historical accounts,
works of poetry, great literature. Many people only ever
read them and understand them on this level. It is only when
the Holy Spirit comes to dwell within a person that the
scriptures really come to life; and when Christians are
baptized and confirmed, they receive the gifts of the Holy
Spirit in fulfilment of that famous prophecy of Isaiah which
is read in Advent: 'A shoot springs from the stock of Jesse, a
scion thrusts from his roots: on him [Jesus] the spirit of the
Lord rests, a spirit of *wisdom* and *insight*, a spirit of counsel
and power, a spirit of knowledge and of the fear of the Lord'

(Isaiah 11:1–2). We who receive the Spirit of God into our lives are given wisdom and understanding when we approach the word of God. In other words we not only have a personal teacher to reveal what the Bible is saying to us, that teacher also happens to be the author!

'Why', you may be thinking at this point, 'if it's that easy, do I not understand some of it?' There are two reasons why the word of God doesn't always get through to people. One is that the gifts are given but not used: they simply don't want to hear it and will not allow it to reach them. Unfortunately this state of affairs is not confined to non-believers: practising Christians, even ministers of the word, can refuse to really take the word to themselves. If a preacher is allowing the word of God to touch his life, then his preaching is alive and communicates life. If he's not, his sermons are like dry bones.

The other reason we sometimes don't understand certain parts of the scriptures is because our teacher, the Holy Spirit, in his wisdom deals with us where we are in our own personal spiritual journey: the bits we don't grasp now are the bits we're not yet ready for. A child cannot learn to read until it knows the alphabet. When it does it can begin to put words together and, eventually, if it continues to learn it can go on to English exams or even a degree—though this will require a great deal of commitment. The Holy Spirit School of Scripture calls for the same: the more we are committed to learn the more he will be able to teach us, especially if we respond to what he is teaching us and always remain *open*. Tomorrow we'll consider the parable of the sower and the various degrees of openness we can display.

Prayer

> *A pure heart create for me, O God,*
> *put a steadfast spirit within me.*
> *Do not cast me away from your presence,*
> *nor deprive me of your holy spirit.*
> *(Psalm 51 [50] : 10–11)*

The Sower and the Word   *Lent 3/Wednesday*

'What the sower is sowing is the word. Those on the
edge of the path where the word is sown are people
who have no sooner heard it than Satan comes and
carries away the word that was sown in them. Similarly,
those who receive the seed on patches of rock are
people who, when first they hear the word, welcome it
at once with joy. But they have no root in them, they do
not last; should some trial come, or some persecution
on account of the word, they fall away at once. Then
there are others who receive the seed in thorns. These
have heard the word, but the worries of this world, the
lure of riches and all the other passions come in to
choke the word, and so it produces nothing. And there
are those who have received the seed in rich soil: they
hear the word and accept it and yield a harvest, thirty
and sixty and a hundredfold.'

(Mark 4:14–20)

In his explanation of the famous parable of the sower Jesus
mentions 'the word' no less than eight times, thereby
emphasizing its importance. The parable itself ends with
that plaintive and familiar plea to the crowds, which seems
to come right from his heart: 'Listen, anyone who has ears to
hear!' And indeed, on the surface of it, the explanation of the
parable is all about hearing—about those who do hear the
word and those who do not.

Yet if we tease out the deeper level of meaning, it actually
has little to do with hearing. All the people mentioned *hear*
the word, but what the parable is really about is *understanding* the word. When people begin to understand the
word of God and accept it, it elicits a response and that
response is always repentance and conversion: such people
are willing to face up to self-revelation, to understand their
own sinfulness and need of forgiveness, to change course

and be forgiven, and ultimately to allow the word to bear fruit in their lives.

Let's just have a look at that list of obstacles preventing people from understanding the word. Foremost is God's arch-enemy, Satan. If we have no sooner heard something than we forget it, that suggests to me a preoccupied mind caught up in what Newman called 'the fever of life', with no time to pause and ponder on what the word is saying. Yet God's power is greater than Satan's, and anyone who really wishes to defeat the enemy can simply change their minds (repent), and say, 'Right, as from now I *will* spend thirty minutes a day reading and reflecting on the gospels'. Let me, at this point, add a personal note. When I was being taught how to read the scriptures prayerfully for an hour a day, the first decision I had to make was that this was going to be a priority and some other activities would have to go. Then once the time has been allocated, the next step is to take pencil and paper and write down the enemy's suggestions for alternative uses of your time (because he'll be working overtime trying to get you to work overtime!). This is how it goes: first I must just phone my publisher . . . I must peel the potatoes . . . must just listen to the news . . . and so on. Then consider the list. Is there anything on it that (*a*) is more important than my relationship with God, and (*b*) can't wait one hour? Of course not, and I can also testify that once you're committed to this, the enemy's tactics cease and you can dispense with pencil and paper!

To move on to the second group—the people who hear the word with joy but it doesn't take root. These are those who don't allow the word to get to them because they think it might cause discomfort. It might be, if they are very egotistic, they are afraid to let go of their self-interest and become vulnerable to God—the Pharisees' problem in fact. They lived with the word of God, their lives were founded on it, yet it never actually touched them. But the gospel testifies to one particular member of the Sanhedrin, 'a teacher in Israel' and an important leader of the Jews, who was a shining example of someone who knew the scriptures through and through yet was humble enough to realize there was a deeper understanding that he did not possess. So he goes to Jesus late at night to ask for help, and is told that if he is willing to be 'born again' in the Spirit he will understand who Jesus is and will inherit eternal life. Nicodemus is an encouraging model of an open mind.

The last negative group are those caught up in ambitions that exclude God, who are too busy chasing wealth or power, whose efforts are concentrated on worldly achievement. Their case is tough but they are not irretrievable. Later in Mark's gospel Jesus adds a positive note: when the bewildered disciples ask 'who could be saved' if it was easier for a camel to pass through the eye of a needle, Jesus simply says that for men it is impossible, but nothing is impossible for God (Mark 10:20). And let us not forget that Paul himself was caught up in a power-battle when he was struck down on the road to Damascus.

Finally in the parable we have the ultimate triumph of the word over Satan and all opposition. Those who do accept and understand it may only be a small proportion of all those who are given the opportunity—but they yield a rich harvest, even a hundredfold. As we read earlier in Isaiah: 'the word of God succeeds in what it was sent to do'.

Prayer
> *In the scroll of the book it stands written*
> *that I should do your will.*
> *My God, I delight in your law*
> *in the depth of my heart.*
> (Psalm 40 [39] : 7–8)

The instructive word   *Lent 3 / Thursday*

Ever since you were a child you have known the holy
scriptures—from these you can learn the wisdom that
leads to salvation through faith in Christ Jesus. All
scripture is inspired by God and can profitably be used
for teaching, for refuting error, for guiding people's
lives and teaching them to be holy. This is how the man
who is dedicated to God becomes fully equipped and
ready for any good work.

(2 Timothy 3:15–17)

This is a wonderfully encouraging text, especially for those
who feel, as I felt at one time, that they are in need of more
teaching. One of the most joyful aspects of discovering
scripture at a deeper level is to find that it contains all the
teaching we will ever need. It is a deep well of information
and inspiration that never runs dry. The more we grow in
our knowledge of scripture, the more it can teach us.

The context of the above letter from Paul to Timothy
(who was in Ephesus) is that there were currently several
new theories and cults floating around, and Paul is warning
Timothy to be faithful to the scripture, which has ultimately
the capacity to discern and refute error. Scripture is a
double-edged sword: not only does it influence individuals, it is also an effective means of forming and shaping
Christian communities in their growth in faith and holiness.

Now, at the end of the twentieth century, the Christian
community is confronted by just the same divisive and
opposing trends that faced Timothy and the church at
Ephesus. The world seems populated with prophets, gurus
and weird sects, hawking leaflets and employing intensive
brainwashing programmes: new messiahs are promoted
with million-dollar advertising campaigns. The tragedy is
that many families experience great distress through the loss
of loved ones who join such movements, and countless
people who have never been fortunate enough to be

instructed in any kind of faith or hope in God are (especially if their lives are already broken) extremely vulnerable to these kinds of influence.

Some movements even claim to be vaguely Christian, which helps to give them a gloss of authenticity. But, for true Christians, St Paul emphasizes one important fact, and that is that *all* scripture is inspired by God. Here is the yardstick by which to measure new theories: bits and pieces of scripture extracted and re-assembled are not the inspired truth of God. Only in the totality of scripture in its full context can we learn the wisdom that leads to faith and salvation. A scripture teacher I know once went to an introductory meeting of one of these movements claiming to be Christian: during the evening she asked to see a copy of their 'Bible', only to discover that it consisted of a patch-work of authentic Bible texts which were thereby rendered totally inauthentic.

Contrast this with Paul's words of encouragement and the immense benefits which accrue from absorbing God's word *as we have received it*. Scripture teaches. Scripture refutes error. Scripture guides people's lives. Scripture teaches us to be holy. Scripture equips us to cope with all aspects of life.

Prayer

> *Entrust your cares to the Lord*
> *and he will support you.*
> *He will never allow*
> *the just man to stumble . . .*
>
> *O Lord, I will trust in you.*
> (Psalm 55 [54] : 22–23)

65

The living word   *Lent 3 / Friday*

The word of God is something alive and active: it cuts
like any double-edged sword but more finely: it can slip
through the place where the soul is divided from the
spirit, or joints from the marrow; it can judge the secret
emotions and thoughts. No created thing can hide
from him; everything is uncovered and open to the
eyes of the one to whom we must give account of
ourselves.

(Hebrews 4:12–13)

The author of the letter to the Hebrews is writing to a new
Jewish/Christian community, and in speaking of the word
here he is referring to *all* that is revealed through the
prophets and through Jesus 'the word made flesh'. For me
these verses are amongst the most significant, because here
we have the word speaking about the word, explaining what
it is and what it does.

When the word of God is spoken things happen; when
people open their eyes and hearts to receive the word of God
they cannot remain unchanged, because it begins to affect
them—it begins to 'act'. The parable of the yeast in the
dough illustrates this very powerfully. If you make an
unleavened dough, what you will have is a mixture of flour
and water: it will feel like a large heavy lump, quite dull and
lifeless. If you add yeast (which is alive and active) and begin
to work at the dough by pummelling it (that is, putting a bit
of effort into it!) very quickly you will find it springing back.
You feel that it comes to life and, soon, it will be so alive that
if you try to make an impression in it with your thumb you
won't be able to because that impression will spring back
into a smooth surface. As the dough rises and increases in
volume it becomes something life-giving.

I could go on—the spiritual analogies of breadmaking are
endless. But suffice it to say that a bag of flour that stays on
the shelf has nothing to offer; but if it is given water (grace),

yeast (the word) and the fire of the oven (the Holy Spirit) it will be transformed into a substance that can feed and sustain life.

In the rest of the above text we are shown another aspect of this living word of God—its power to penetrate and touch our deepest thoughts and feelings. Here I think it's interesting, and important, to note that the writer starts off by referring to the word as the word, but finishes up calling it Him ('no created thing can hide from him'). At the Last Supper Jesus pointed ahead to the Holy Spirit who will 'teach you and remind you of all I have said'. When we receive the Holy Spirit, he in turn points back to Jesus: allowing the word to penetrate our lives will bring us closer to the person of Jesus in an intimate one-to-one relationship. It is Jesus that no created thing can hide from, but this need not be a frightening or daunting prospect. The writer goes on to explain that Jesus has, through his humanity, experienced *all* the weaknesses we do, that he has been tempted in all the ways we are.

Because we have a high priest in heaven who *knows* what it is like to be human, we can confidently approach him and be sure of finding help. So to sum up: we must not be afraid to let the word of God penetrate our hidden thoughts or the dark areas of our lives, because Jesus understands them and will provide us with all the grace and help we need. There would, after all, be no point in God sending us a saviour if we didn't have anything to be saved from! In this context let us pray again the prayer of the psalmist:

> *O search me, God, and know my heart.*
> *O test me and know my thoughts.*
> *See that I follow not the wrong path*
> *and lead me in the path of life eternal.*
>
> (Psalm 139 [138] : 23–24)

The recipe for faith   *Lent 3/Saturday*

'If you make my word your home you will indeed be my
disciples, you will learn the truth and the truth will make
you free.'

(John 8:31–32)

Within these two short verses is contained a rich summary
of all that a Christian needs for growth in faith, knowledge of
truth and, ultimately, total freedom to be a child of God.

While we, like St Paul, keep straining ahead and running
in the race, what we need to remember is that what we're
running towards is not our goal, but God's. He has only one
desire—to establish his kingdom here on earth as it is in
heaven. This is what we pray for each day, this kingdom in
which his children will be at last totally free of sin and death,
free from pain, sorrow and suffering. When we pray for the
coming of the kingdom what we are praying for is God's
final plan of that new heaven and new earth portrayed so
vividly in the Book of Revelation: 'Here God lives *among*
men. He will make his home among them; and they shall be
his people, and he will be their God; his name is God-with-
them. He will wipe away all tears from their eyes; there will
be no more death, and no more mourning or sadness. The
world of the past has gone' (Revelation 21:3–4).

We are the pilgrim people of God journeying through the
wilderness of our earthly lives, and it is here in the humdrum
messiness of our daily lives that he is preparing us for his
kingdom. As he explains to the people of the Exodus (the
Bible's allegory for the journey of the spiritual life): 'I led
you through the wilderness to humble you, to test you, to
know your inmost heart ... I was training you as a man
trains his child ... to keep the commandments of God, to
follow his ways and to reverence him'. And speaking of their
trials the Lord has this to say: 'He humbled you, he made
you feel hunger ... to make you understand that man does
not live on bread alone' but on every word that proceeds

from the mouth of God (Deuteronomy 8:3).

Which brings us back to today's text and the fundamental need for every Christian to feed on the word of God daily. 'If you make my word your home . . . ' Notice the 'if' clause which precedes all of God's promises. If you are really serious about letting the gospel message reach that deep centre of yourself (not just a haphazard dip here and there, but spending time reading and reflecting on the whole of each gospel), 'you will indeed be my disciple'. Not just a Christian, note, not even a committed Christian, but a disciple. And a disciple, as we understand it, is not just a pupil but someone who has a close relationship with his teacher. Jesus is saying, 'You will indeed be someone whom I will teach *and* have a close relationship with'.

There is another promise. 'You will learn the truth'—the truth about oneself, about life, about God—and as we learn the truth so it will set us free. A clear and decisive statement, not that it might or could set us free, but it *will*. The truth will set us free from whatever binds and constricts us: if we want to be fully alive, to stretch out our wings and soar like eagles high above the things that imprison us, here in this short text is how Jesus, the word made flesh, God-with-us, was sent to 'bring the good news to the poor, to proclaim liberty to captives' (Luke 4:18).

Prayer

> *In God alone is my soul at rest;*
> *my help comes from him.*
> *He alone is my rock, my stronghold,*
> *my fortress: I stand firm.*
>
> *(Psalm 62 [61] : 1–2)*

Prayer

The commandment of love

Listen, Israel: The Lord our God is the one Lord. You shall love the Lord your God with all your heart, with all your soul, and with all your strength. Let these words I urge on you today be written on your heart. You shall repeat them to your children and say them over to them, whether at rest in your house or walking abroad, at your lying down or at your rising . . .

(Deuteronomy 6:4–7)

Sometimes, in order to understand the wonder of God's plan and of his relationship with us, his creatures, it is necessary to understand his utter simplicity as well. God communicates through his word (scripture) and through his creation (nature), but either way the message is simple. Let us consider today's passage.

The definitions of divine love and its human response we can leave to the theologians, but to *understand* them we can find a simple parallel in nature—the love of a man for a woman and the path of its growth. Let's say it begins with a mutual attraction drawing two people towards each other; this can develop into a flirtation, light-hearted even casual, in which the attraction begins to be communicated. If it grows, other relationships would begin to cease and the two people start the process of getting to know one another. This might take months or years, but eventually the relationship would become what we call 'serious', as the first shallow 'love-at-first-sight' emotions are replaced by a more mature growth in love.

What happens next is a commitment—a marriage contract. The couple decide to go forward and commit themselves to loving one another for life. Although feelings and emotions are involved, the ultimate decision is one of the will. Thus the responses by the couple during the marriage service are simply 'I will'. I will love . . .

It is this very decision to love that God is asking of his people in the first commandment and (as we are told) it is no small commitment: it is one that should be 'written on our hearts' and be observed in every aspect of our daily lives, not just at prayer-time or in church worship. At the beginning of our relationship with God we sense that we're being drawn to him; our interest may be casual at first but as it grows, we begin to seek, then we begin to find, then we begin to know him, then we begin to love him.

Thus prayer is a commitment first to knowing, and then to loving. A young couple can't really begin to love one another deeply until they really know one another. In the same way our response to the first commandment should be an acknowledgement that we need to *learn* how to obey it, how to really love God. The first step in prayer is to know Jesus personally in a one-to-one relationship—the Good Shepherd, you will recall, called his sheep *one by one* ('my sheep know my voice'). The lambs who stay near the shepherd all the time get to know his voice so well that they are able to follow him closely always (see John 10:14–16).

The most important factor in any relationship is, quite simply, time. To relate to a person it is essential to spend time with them. As Lent is a time of challenge, let us respond fully to this challenge, committing ourselves to a deeper relationship with God by saying 'I will'. I will find time every day to reflect on the word of God, getting to know Jesus better in order to see through him the reflection of God the Father, and through the power of the Holy Spirit to learn to love God with *all* my heart and with *all* my mind and with *all* my strength.

Prayer

> *O Lord, you have been our refuge*
> *from one generation to the next.*
> *Before the mountains were born*
> *or the earth or the world brought forth,*
> *you are God, without beginning or end.*

(Psalm 90 [89] : 1–2)

Choosing prayer   *Lent 4 / Monday*

Now Martha who was distracted with all the serving said, 'Lord, do you not care that my sister is leaving me to do the serving all by myself?' . . . 'Martha, Martha,' he said, 'you worry and fret about so many things, and yet few are needed, indeed only one. It is Mary who has chosen the better part.'

(Luke 10:40–42)

I think the very first thing we have to consider about this story is where Luke has placed it. So often gospel stories and teachings are extracted and cited on their own, when in fact they have a much richer meaning if seen in context. I feel that this particular, much-quoted story has sometimes suffered from this. I suppose it's rather like looking at a recipe made up of several ingredients—on their own they won't provide anything like the results they will when put together.

We should start at the point (v. 25) where Jesus is asked by a lawyer what he must do to inherit eternal life. He turns the question back on the man with another question: What is written in the Law? The lawyer answers by quoting

73

Deuteronomy (see yesterday's notes), 'You must love the Lord your God with all your heart', adding the second great commandment, 'Love your neighbour as yourself'. Do this, Jesus says, and life is yours. The man asks then, Who is my neighbour? Jesus replies with the well-known story of the Good Samaritan (which as we know is all about caring for others). It is after this that Luke tells us about Martha and Mary—and after that Jesus teaches the disciples how to pray.

The point I'm trying to make is this: if we take the story of the Good Samaritan on its own it can sound as if loving your neighbour is *the* most important part of being a Christian. Similarly if the Martha and Mary story is taken on its own it can give the impression that loving in a prayerful contemplative way is somehow vastly superior to loving in works of service. Elsewhere Jesus himself said that the whole of the Law can be summed up in the two commandments 'Love the Lord your God with all your heart... and love your neighbour as yourself' (Matthew 22:34–40). But they are inseparable: while it is true that loving God is number one on the list it cannot be separated from number two.

However, to return to Martha, who the gospel tells us was an intimate friend of Jesus along with her sister Mary and brother Lazarus. What we are invited in on here is not a specific teaching-session, but a relaxed social evening. Martha, we read, 'welcomed him into her house': she was warm and receptive. My personal belief is that what Jesus was saying to her was, You are rushing about trying to do *too* much, you don't need to be busy with so many activities. He's not saying, Give up active service; he's saying, Give up *over*-active service and learn to sit and listen to me like Mary. The reason this is the better part is because in seeking God in prayer and in listening to his word, we will discover that he himself is the inspirer and initiator of our service. Thus if Martha listens to God in prayer she won't become over-burdened. 'Come to me' (our Lord himself said in Matthew 11:28–29) 'all you who labour and are overburdened... learn from me.'

To sum up, someone who has a prayer-life will be more sensitive to the real needs of others. Someone who is 'coming to' the Lord in prayer and learning from him will not have to 'worry and fret about too many things when few are needed'. So today if we read and meditate on Luke 10: 25–42, the Good Samaritan will teach us about caring for others, while Martha will remind us not to over-do our caring so that we have no time to pray. And from Mary we will learn that being still and listening to the word of God is of paramount importance if we are to grow—both in our love of God and in our caring for others.

Prayer

> *I will hear what the Lord God has to say,*
> *a voice that speaks of peace,*
> *peace for his people and his friends*
> *and those who turn to him in their hearts.*
>
> *(Psalm 85 [84] : 8)*

Teach us to pray   *Lent 4 / Tuesday*

> Now once he was in a certain place praying, and when he had finished one of his disciples said, 'Lord, teach us to pray ...'
>
> *(Luke 11:1)*

Having illustrated the importance of prayer with the story of Martha and Mary, Luke next brings us to a scene where Jesus is teaching the disciples *how* to pray. As the disciples were Jewish, both private and corporate prayer were firmly rooted in their religion, but I think we can assume that they probably hadn't had a great deal of success with personal prayer—hence their eagerness to learn. They knew that John the Baptist had taught his disciples to pray, and by now

75

they had often observed Jesus himself going off to pray quietly. So they must have guessed its importance and were anxious to learn.

If we too are anxious to learn, we must look once again at Jesus the man. One thing that emerges clearly from the gospels is the number of times Jesus goes off to pray. There is a discipline about prayer in his life which is an object lesson for us. His life was full of activity, teaching and healing: he was constantly followed by huge crowds and was in great demand at meals and social occasions—but in spite of all these pressures prayer still dominated his life. We hear of him getting up early to pray, for instance; and after the feeding of the five thousand he dismissed the crowd and 'went up into the hills by himself to pray' (Matthew 14:23).

Our first objective, before we can even begin to learn to pray, is to learn how to be like him and find the *time* for prayer. It requires the kind of discipline that modern life seldom allows for—but just think how hard it must have been for *him* to turn his back on people's very pressing needs and go off to pray. What we have to do is imitate him, and learn to find some time in our daily lives for God.

The first step is to question some of our own attitudes. For myself it has taken me quite a long time to discover how dispensable I am, and how well able the Lord is to care and provide for people without any help from me. That's not to say I've become redundant in Christian service, but I've learnt to seek God's blessing first in all I do. In this respect the wise words of the psalmist have been most helpful: 'If the Lord does not build the house, in vain do its builders labour; if the Lord does not watch over the city, in vain does the watchman keep vigil. In vain is your earlier rising, your going later to rest, you who toil for the bread you eat: when he pours gifts on his beloved while they slumber' (Psalm 127 [126]:1–2).

Let the words of the psalmist speak to us as we reflect on how to find the time for prayer. Question how much of what we do is what the Lord is asking of us, and how much is keeping up to our own (or the world's) standards.

Remember the words of Jesus when he said, '*My* yoke is easy, and *my* burden light'. Sometimes the burdens we put on ourselves are so difficult—we can be subconsciously striving to save the world ourselves, instead of allowing our Lord to be the saviour. Let us pray for the wisdom to get our priorities right, to give time to a prayerful relationship that will initiate and bless all that we do.

Prayer

> *It is you whom I invoke, O Lord.*
> *In the morning you hear me;*
> *in the morning I offer you my prayer,*
> *watching and waiting.*
>
> (Psalm 5:3)

A secret place   *Lent 4/Wednesday*

'But when you pray, go to your private room and, when you have shut your door, pray to your Father who is in that secret place . . . '

(Matthew 6:6)

Both Luke and Matthew describe the scene where Jesus is instructing the disciples on prayer. In Matthew we hear about the dangers of hypocrisy (v. 5), the unnecessary use of 'many words' (v. 7), and the importance of personal one-to-one prayer with God.

Hypocrites are those who keep up the outward show of religion while their hearts are far from God—throughout scripture hypocrisy is abhorrent to God and we can detect a tone of anger when Jesus describes them and says, 'I tell you solemnly, they have had their reward'. At the same time we are told it is quite unnecessary to make long and elaborate prayers, 'to babble and use many words'. The disciples have to grasp that God is all-knowing; they do not have to include a whole catalogue of background information and minor detail, or rationalize their requests. God already knows everything.

One point that needs a mention here (and we'll be discussing in detail later on) is that this is not a case against corporate prayer. Jesus himself took part in public worship in synagogues and the temple. The instructions above are concerned with private prayer as an *addition* to public worship, not instead of.

I've often heard it said you don't have to go on your knees to pray, that you can pray at any time, on the bus, walking the dog, washing the dishes. With that I would certainly agree, and indeed add that sometimes God seems most manifest in various aspects of his creation, in beautiful landscapes, in the sound of the sea, in music, architecture—the list is endless—and it would be foolish to suggest that awareness of God can be confined to prayer-time. But it is quite clear from Jesus' own life and from these particular instructions that those kinds of moments are a supplement to, not a substitute for, personal prayer.

So what about this place of prayer, this private room? One writer, I recall, said that this private place was inside ourselves, in our hearts. We didn't have to go physically into a quiet place, we could just mentally withdraw. It may sound feasible, but in my experience unless a person is especially holy they would find it extremely difficult to come to quiet in the presence of God whilst surrounded by noise and distractions. (It is an attitude, I would suggest, that comes either from saints or from those who are making an excuse to avoid the whole issue of this personal relationship with God.)

Therefore for beginners like me I would strongly recommend a physical quiet place where we can do exactly what our Lord said, shut the door on the world for a specific time each day and be in the presence of our heavenly Father. We live in a world of high speed and much noise, and we are vulnerable to every kind of medium of communication imposing their hidden pressures on us. The reason so many tranquillizers are prescribed is because people have forgotten how to be tranquil.

Once again we can reflect on one of the psalms (46 [45]). This particular psalm sums up the quietude of prayer: 'Be still and know that I am God, supreme among the nations, supreme on the earth!' When Elijah went up to the mountain to stand before God, the experience was not as he imagined. He discovered God was not in the mighty wind, or in the earthquake or in the fire, but in the sound of the gentle breeze or the still small voice within (1 Kings 16:12). Those caught up in the noisy fever of life will not hear this still small voice within unless they learn to be still themselves, to come into a secret place, close the door and learn to be still and *know* God.

Prayer
> *I will bless the Lord who gives me counsel,*
> *who even at night directs my heart.*
> *I keep the Lord ever in my sight:*
> *since he is at my right hand, I shall stand firm.*
> *(Psalm 16 [15] : 7–8)*

God's guarantee   *Lent 4 / Thursday*

'So I say to you: Ask, and it will be given to you; search, and you will find; knock, and the door will be opened to you. For the one who asks always receives; the one who searches always finds; the one who knocks will always have the door opened.'

(Luke 11:9–10)

It is just before this passage in Luke that Jesus has taught the disciples the 'Our Father'. Separated out, the 'Our Father' can be seen as a list of the essential themes of prayer:

reverence for God and acknowledgement of his holiness; a prayer for the kingdom to be established where God's will will be accomplished; asking for God to provide for our daily needs; asking for forgiveness—and understanding our own need to forgive others; asking for help to face the inevitable temptations, the choice between good and evil that confront us every day; then the final plea for deliverance from the evil influences that surround us.

The closer we come to God and the more we grow in prayer, the better we begin to understand our heartfelt need to pray through this essential list. After the 'Our Father', Jesus goes on to emphasize the importance of the word *ask*. Reading the whole of Luke's account of Jesus' teaching on prayer (vv. 1–13), it seems to me three important points are underlined: (*a*) we must understand our real needs as opposed to what we think our needs are; (*b*) the story of the importunate friend to me illustrates perseverance in learning to pray, in prayer itself, and in learning to relate to God in a personal way so that we can really receive all we want (because it will be *all* that God wants to give us). This is borne out absolutely by (*c*): if we persist in asking, the answers will be given; if we persist in seeking God, we're sure of finding him; if we persist in our desire to learn, and knock on doors with question-marks on them, they'll be opened.

Notice all this is absolutely *guaranteed*—Jesus is emphatic. But what he is guaranteeing is something much greater than merely standing before God in prayer and asking him for the money to send Granny to Australia. He may well provide it, *but* the request in itself is paltry compared with what's really being offered when we seek God in prayer. Whoever perseveres, keeps knocking on the door of faith, will begin to have access to the very thoughts and ways of God himself. As Paul says in the letter to the Corinthians, 'we have [taken on] the mind of Christ' (1 Corinthians 2:16).

It's in this context that we begin to grasp our own real needs (and those of others), because Jesus himself will teach us what to pray for. This we have been assured of in his own

words, when he spoke elsewhere of the material needs of
people: 'Your heavenly Father knows your needs', he said.
'Set your hearts on his kingdom *first* . . . and all these other
things will be given you *as well*' (Matthew 6:33).

Prayer

> *There is one thing I ask for of the Lord,*
> *for this I long,*
> *to live in the house of the Lord,*
> *all the days of my life,*
> *to savour the sweetness of the Lord,*
> *to behold his temple.*
>
> *(Psalm 27 [26] : 4)*

No hiding-place from God   *Lent 4/Friday*

O Lord, you search me and you know me,
you know my resting and my rising,
you discern my purpose from afar.
You mark when I walk or lie down,
all my ways lie open to you.

Before ever a word is on my tongue
you know it, O Lord, through and through.
Behind and before you besiege me,
your hand ever laid upon me.
Too wonderful for me, this knowledge,
too high, beyond my reach.

O where can I go from your spirit,
or where can I flee from your face?
If I climb the heavens, you are there.
If I lie in the grave, you are there.

(Psalm 139 [138] : 1–8)

During this week we have considered a few aspects of prayer: the first commandment to love God with all our capacity for loving; to understand the necessity of sitting quietly; learning to be still and ask for this relationship of love to grow within us. The words of today's psalm illustrate most beautifully the reality of the situation in prayer between God and us—inasmuch as it is he who does the seeking.

God pursues every one of his creatures through the whole of their lives—he is behind and before them, his hand ever laid on them. Remember Jeremiah: 'when you seek me with all your heart, I will let you find me' (29:13–14). God longs to let us find him, and he is permanently there—(as the Book of Deuteronomy expresses so vividly) 'Like an eagle watching its nest, hovering over its young' (32:11). I learned only recently that when an eaglet is being taught to fly, his mother pushes him off a cliff-edge and then hovers over him as he learns to use his wings. If he gets into difficulty she swoops down underneath, so that he can fall safely onto her outstretched wings!

This image of God's parental love for his children is echoed by Isaiah: 'Does a woman forget her baby at the breast, or fail to cherish the son of her womb? Yet even if these forget, I will never forget you. See, I have branded you on the palms of my hands' (49:15–16). Ezekiel (ch. 34) develops the theme of eternal remembrance—for God himself is the true shepherd who 'looks for the lost one, brings back the stray, bandages the wounded and makes the weak strong'. And to quote perhaps the most lyrical of all the pictures of God seeking out his loved ones, from the Song of Songs: 'Come then, my love, my lovely one, come. My dove, hiding in the clefts of the rock, in the coverts of the cliff, show me your face, let me hear your voice; for your voice is sweet and your face is beautiful' (2:13–14).

Can we not see ourselves in this picture if we look closely? God calls us to his close relationship with him in prayer, but we are hiding. The clefts of the rock are our human pretensions, ambitions, pride and intellect. Why? Because deep-down we are afraid we have no value. Perhaps my voice isn't at all sweet nor my face beautiful, and perhaps I am in some way responsible . . .

The psalmist has appreciated that he cannot hide from God: 'For it was you who created my being, knit me together in my mother's womb . . . Already you knew my soul, my body held no secret from you'. Knowing this, he is able to praise God for his own creation: 'I thank you for the wonder of my being!' When God calls us out of our hiding-place and we start to listen and let him love us, then secure in the knowledge of that love we will be able not only to face ourselves but actually to learn to love ourselves. Gradually we can be healed of the effects of sin and be restored to our full potential—so that we too can thank him for the wonder of our being.

Prayer

> *O Lord, I cried to you for help*
> *and you, my God, have healed me.*
> *O Lord, you have raised my soul from the dead.*
> *restored me to life from those who sink into the grave.*
>
> (Psalm 30 [29] : 2–3)

Prayer and loving   *Lent 4 / Saturday*

This, then, is what I pray, kneeling before the Father, from whom every family, whether spiritual or natural, takes its name:

Out of his infinite glory, may he give you the power through his Spirit for your hidden self to grow strong, so that Christ may live in your hearts through faith, and then, planted in love and built on love, you will with all the saints have strength to grasp the breadth and the length, the height and the depth; until, knowing the love of Christ, which is beyond all knowledge, you are filled with the utter fullness of God.

Glory be to him whose power, working in us, can do infinitely more than we can ask or imagine; glory be to him from generation to generation in the Church and in Christ Jesus for ever and ever. Amen.

(Ephesians 3:14–21)

Perhaps one of the reasons I love scripture so much is because I have an innate love of words: poetry, literature, any form of communication through words fascinates me. My passport describes me as a journalist and for many years I have attempted to communicate the art of cookery through the written word. Maybe that's why when I read the letters of St Paul I am almost over-awed at his ability to communicate so powerfully and precisely. This immensely beautiful prayer is a gem. It was written for the people of the church at Ephesus, but as part of holy scripture it remains a prayer for all time for those who are seeking God.

For me, this prayer is not only asking for, but literally describing, all that happens to people when they begin to have a prayer-life, a time set aside for a relationship with God. Things *do* start to happen. Through the power of the Holy Spirit there is new birth and new life of the 'hidden self' (which we have described elsewhere as the deepest centre). Then the hidden self begins to grow and, as the prayer-life continues, so does the growth, like a plant beginning to blossom and its delicate flower beginning to open.

This tiny flower is the inner self awakening to love, or rather I should say, beginning to learn how to love. Prayer is a school for loving: it is in this prayer-relationship that we learn how to love God, how to love ourselves, and how to love others—which Jesus said summed up the whole of God's law ('Love the Lord your God with all your heart and love your neighbour *as yourself*'). We cannot love ourselves until we have experienced God's love for us, and if we haven't learned to love ourselves we cannot really give ourselves in love to others.

Prayer time, then, is a time for learning about love and, as we grow stronger, so our vision of love will open out, enabling us in the end to 'know what is beyond all knowledge . . . and be filled with the utter fullness of God'. God's power will give us the capacity to do more than we ever imagined, and the fruits of prayer will flow out to bless others.

Prayer

> *Like the deer that yearns*
> *for running streams,*
> *so my soul is yearning*
> *for you, my God.*
>
> *My soul is thirsting for God,*
> *the God of my life;*
> *when can I enter and see*
> *the face of God?*
>
> (Psalm 42 [41] : 1–2)

Growth

'Come to me, all you who labour and are overburdened, and I will give you rest. Shoulder my yoke and learn from me, for I am gentle and humble in heart, and you will find rest for your souls. Yes, my yoke is easy and my burden light.'

(Matthew 11:28–30)

These words of Jesus seem to span the centuries and speak very directly to the people of today, who suffer greatly from a modern disease called speed. Sometimes we can become completely overburdened with physical activity: we get caught on a kind of treadmill, like a hamster running furiously with the wheel turning faster and faster but getting nowhere.

Stress is said to be a contributory factor in many modern diseases, and it's my own belief that noise causes and aggravates stress. We not only have radios and televisions in our homes, we have car radios, personal walking stereo systems, piped music in shopping centres and supermarkets, restaurants and pubs. It is little wonder that people go to their doctors in desperate need asking for tranquillizers, which in the end can only patch up like sticking-plasters, but never heal the problem.

There is a line in Mark's gospel that epitomizes the message of Lent for me: 'You must come away to some lonely place all by yourselves and rest for a while'. Why did Jesus say this? Because 'there were so many coming and going that the apostles had no time even to eat' (Mark 6:31). Lent is a time to get off the treadmill, to examine our situation. Being burdened with normal daily activities, hard work, providing for or running a home, bringing up a family is one thing; but being *over*-burdened is quite another. If we are too pressured this puts strains on our health and on our relationships and, above all, is a huge block to growth in faith and knowledge of God.

Sometimes the burdens that people are carrying around are in the name of God, whom they have quite misunderstood: 'I must measure up to all that my friends or relations or colleagues expect me to be'. Any attempt to opt out or back down will result in crippling guilt. So I give in to the demands that are made on me in an attempt to placate this peculiar imagined God. It's as though loving my neighbour were something that can be accomplished by flexed muscles, gritted teeth and a very determined effort. Those around this sort of person know perfectly well that you only flog a willing horse. So they flog, and the treadmill keeps turning.

But Jesus has something to say to people on the treadmill. ' "Come to me . . . learn from me." Let me teach you how to love your neighbour, and then you'll find my teaching will make the whole process easier. Why? Because I will teach you how to really feel love, to give to others easily and naturally. I can teach you to say "No" when it's right to say "No", without feeling guilt. "My yoke is easy and my burden is light." '

Finally, the only words in all the gospel accounts that Jesus uses to describe himself: 'I am gentle and humble in heart'. And that, he's saying, is how I want you to be, gentle and humble. Don't try to become a paragon of virtue like the Pharisee who counted up all his good deeds and thanked God he was so good. It was the publican whose only prayer was 'Be merciful to me, a sinner' (Luke 18:13) who was at rights with God, because he knew how to acknowledge his own weakness. Tomorrow we will discuss this, the greatest challenge to Christian faith, the challenge of true humility.

Prayer
> *It is he who will free you from the snare*
> *of the fowler who seeks to destroy you;*
> *he will conceal you with his pinions*
> *and under his wings you will find refuge.*
>
> *(Psalm 91 [90] : 3–4)*

Know your enemy   *Lent 5/Monday*

God refuses the proud and will always favour the humble. Bow down, then, before the power of God now, and he will raise you up on the appointed day; unload all your worries on to him, since he is looking after you. Be calm but vigilant, because your enemy the devil is prowling round like a roaring lion, looking for someone to eat. Stand up to him, strong in faith and in the knowledge that our brothers all over the world are suffering the same things. You will have to suffer for only a little while: the God of all grace who called you to eternal glory in Christ will see that all is well again: he will confirm, strengthen and support you.

(1 Peter 5:5–10)

This is a wonderfully supportive text, from the first letter of Peter. First of all quoting scripture himself (Proverbs 3:34), he confirms what we have spoken about earlier, the importance of humility. That is, understanding our own weakness and inability to redeem ourselves, and therefore bowing down before the power of God which alone can raise us up to our full human potential.

As he points out, it won't all be plain sailing: we have not yet entered the promised land, we are still pilgrims in the wilderness and there we will encounter the opponent of God's plan for humanity, Satan. We have all the means to resist him, but unless we understand what they are we are vulnerable to attack. Pride is what gives him total access, his inroad to destruction. Eve, in the garden of Eden, was assured by the serpent that if she ate of the tree of knowledge of good and evil she could become like God. Pride came before that first fall, and Satan continues to tempt us through our pride and we continue to fall. History is littered with casualties. Just one—if particularly horrific-example was Hitler, who stirred up a whole nation to act through pride; we still inherit the consequences of that reign of destruction, reminding us of the wages of the sin of pride and the fall that inevitably succeeds it. '

On the other hand Satan simply cannot tempt the humble, because there is no means of temptation. If Adam and Eve had said, 'No thanks, we're *happy* to be only human', Satan would have remained impotent. Which was exactly how Jesus dealt with him (as we read on the first Sunday of Lent): 'I don't *want* all the kingdoms of the earth'. Material things are irrelevant because man's real *need* is God. Jesus became the new Adam, but plunging to the utter depths (if that is the word) of humility as a human being—accused, scourged, mocked, and suffering the lowest form of public execution in crucifixion—he utterly defeated the enemy of all human beings.

Satan's earliest means of communication was a serpent, the most subtle of all creatures, and Satan's subtle approach is to begin by making us feel incomplete in some way, playing on our weakness, making us feel small but all the while cajoling us to want to become tall. The answer is so simple. We must be *content* to be small and pray for an understanding of our nothingness. As Jesus said, 'Without me you can do nothing'. The weakest lambs are the ones who stay closest to the shepherd: close to him they are safe from lions and predators. He cares for the weak one, bandages the wounds of incompleteness, and he makes them strong. 'He will see that all is well', Peter says above. 'He will confirm you, support you and make you strong.'

Prayer
> *Lord God, I take refuge in you.*
> *From my pursuer save me and rescue me,*
> *lest he tear me to pieces like a lion*
> *and drag me off with no one to rescue me.*
> *(Psalm 7:1–2)*

The emptying of self   *Lent 5/Tuesday*

His state was divine, yet he did not cling to his equality with God, but emptied himself, to assume the condition of a slave, and become as men are; and being as all men are, he was humbler yet, even to accepting death, death on a cross. But God raised him high and gave him the name which is above all other names, so that all beings in the heavens, on the earth and in the under-world, should bend the knee at the name of Jesus.

(Philippians 2:6–10)

Jesus is the teacher who teaches humility and gentleness to human beings, not from outside their humanity but from within the very context of the human condition. 'He became as men are ... and was humbler yet.' It is hard to grasp the concept of the humility of God, that he could become like us, sharing our humanity, in order that we might become like him and share his divinity.

All through the Bible humility is emphasized as being the principal virtue, and pride (its opposite) as the deadliest of the sins. 'He has pulled down princes from their thrones and exalted the lowly' (Luke 1:52). Pride it was that caused the rebellion in heaven, pride the fall from the garden of Eden, and pride that ever since separates people from God. When man plays at being God, wanting to be in charge of his own destiny, that is pride at work.

God goes to great lengths to save people from their pride. St Paul was given his famous thorn 'to stop me from getting too proud'. Whatever Paul's thorn might have been, it was there because Paul had to learn that God's power 'is at its best in weakness' (2 Corinthians 12:7–9). For us any growth in faith will only be possible if we can openly come to terms with our great enemy, the ego. And the stark truth is that we would much rather not, we would prefer to keep it hidden, especially from ourselves! I know when I prayed for a deeper faith and knowledge of God, the first thing he did was to let me take a little peep at myself; and what I saw was a mountain of self-centredness!

I believe the first step in humility is to recognize the pride of self, and simply ask God for help. When we realize what we are, and appreciate our absolute weakness, then God can begin the work of raising us up. It takes a lifetime, but only God can accomplish this work, only the Holy Spirit, using the circumstances of our daily lives, can free us from self-interest. But beware, this humbling process cannot be forced or faked: false humility is simply pride in disguise. The person who is protesting about being 'no good' is advertising a need for esteem. True humility is trying to learn to do without it, to be free of needing it.

What we must pray for is the wisdom to learn from Jesus how to be humble, how to submit to this self-emptying, how to say (with John the Baptist), 'He must grow greater, I must grow smaller' (John 3:30).

Prayer

> *Preserve me, God, I take refuge in you.*
> *I say to the Lord: 'You are my God.*
> *My happiness lies in you alone.'*
> *(Psalm 16 [15] : 1–2)*

Discipleship   *Lent 5/Wednesday*

'If anyone wants to be a follower of mine, let him
renounce himself and take up his cross every day and
follow me. For anyone who wants to save his life will
lose it; but anyone who loses his life for my sake, that
man will save it. What gain, then, is it for a man to have
won the whole world and to have lost or ruined his very
self?'

(Luke 9:23–25)

Many people imagine that if they give their lives to God he
will automatically send them some terrible, testing burden,
a heavy 'cross' for them to carry to prove their fidelity.
Likewise, when someone is undergoing some difficulty or
particularly painful situation it is often written off as being a
'cross'—something we just have to sit back and bear the best
we can. For me this kind of hairshirt mentality is not
compatible with the tender loving image of God in the
Bible: it is (I think) a distortion of the real teaching of Jesus
in the above text.

It is an extremely important teaching—all the synoptic
writers record it and John has written a beautiful commentary on it in chapter 12 of his gospel. The text contains the
message which is the touchstone of all authentic Christianity, which is this: being willing to take up my cross means
being prepared to take on the responsibility of facing my
'very self'. If I want to be a follower of Jesus I must allow his
Spirit to reveal me to myself, I must stand in that light of
self-revelation and be willing to renounce (with his help)
everything that's not in harmony with his will. We can flirt
with the Christian message, we can try to find other routes of
growth—but they will be cul-de-sacs and, as a priest I know
once put it, the trouble there is that sooner or later you come
and bump into yourself. There's only one road, and that
leads to Calvary and the cross.

Self-indulgence, self-centredness, self-will, all must be

purified. This is the pilgrim journey of the follower of Christ, which teaches us that to attain the heights of union with God we must first experience the depths of self-surrender. As with the bride in the Song of Songs coming up from the desert leaning on her beloved, Jesus wishes to teach us to stop relying on ourselves and lean on him.

This coming up from the desert is a rising up to new life, every step on the journey to the cross being a step nearer the resurrection. The call to discipleship may indeed be a daunting one, and facing ourselves would be impossible were it not for God's mercy. The road might be hard and narrow, but as we follow it we begin to experience eternal life welling up in the depths of our being, so that we cry out with Mary, 'The Almighty has done great things for me. Holy is his name, and his mercy reaches from age to age for those who fear him' (Luke 1:49). Discipleship is death to self, then, a sacrificial offering whose blessings can flow out to the rest of the world. As Jesus has promised: 'Unless a wheat grain falls on the ground and dies, it remains only a single grain; but if it dies, it yields a rich harvest' (John 12:24).

Prayer

> *O my Strength, it is you to whom I turn,*
> *for you, O God, are my stronghold,*
> *the God who shows me love.*
> (Psalm 59 [58] : 17)

94

The results of self-indulgence   *Lent 5 / Thursday*

Let me put it like this: if you are guided by the Spirit you
will be in no danger of yielding to self-indulgence,
since self-indulgence is the opposite of the Spirit, the
Spirit is totally against such a thing, and it is precisely
because the two are so opposed that you do not
always carry out your good intentions. If you are led by
the Spirit, no law can touch you. When self-indulgence
is at work the results are obvious: fornication, gross
indecency and sexual irresponsibility; idolatry and
sorcery; feuds and wrangling, jealousy, bad temper
and quarrels; disagreements, factions, envy,
drunkenness, orgies and similar things. I warn you now,
as I warned you before: those who behave like this will
not inherit the kingdom of God.

(Galatians 5:16–21)

I once read an article by a prominent Anglican clergyman
which emphasized the dangers of complacency in the
Christian life—how if we're not careful we can manufac-
ture in our minds a 'sugar-coated gospel'. I agree with what
he said, and admit to being aware in myself of the dangers of
dwelling on the soft options, of taking to heart the beautiful
promises of Jesus whilst ignoring the 'if' clauses. The
people of Israel journeying through the wilderness had
the same problem: they kept wanting to settle where they
were. When you find a cool oasis in the desert, the promised
land might seem like an awful lot of bother. But God kept
moving them on, because he knew that the promised land
could offer them more than they ever dreamed of. So it is
with our spiritual journey. God wants to move us on all the
time, and in order to grow spiritually we need to be
challenged constantly.

Chapter 5 of Galatians is full of challenges, both to
communities and to individuals. It compares side by side
the fruits of self-indulgence (above) with the harvest of the

Spirit (tomorrow's reading). If there was a top twenty of favourite scripture passages I'm sure the one above would not be on it, but taken together with tomorrow's reading it does offer a challenge, a means to gauge our spiritual temperature, as it were. It's doubtful whether any one of us (certainly not me) could dismiss the entire list as not applicable. We'd have to be extraordinarily holy if we were able to say, I am never jealous, or quarrelsome, or envious, and so on.

Perhaps there are some items on the list we needn't dwell on, but before passing over the first three we might consider them in the light of our modern 'permissive' society. We are constantly being brainwashed with the sexual implications of almost everything, but God created sex (and we thank him profoundly for that gift) not only for the procreation of children but also as an expression of love. The sexual act is the giving of self to a loved one. But once sex is divorced from love it becomes precisely as St Paul says, mere self-indulgence.

Two items on the list we could be tempted to pass over in these modern times, if we don't examine their implications closely: idolatry and sorcery. I've had trouble with both, so let me explain. Sorcery covers anything to do with the occult: fortune-telling, tarot cards, even star-forecasting. Is it not incongruous at one moment to profess faith and trust in God and at the next to be reading the horoscope for the month ahead? St Paul warns us this is self-indulgence, so—even in the small ways—we must learn to be faithful. How about idolatry? We might not be carving graven images nowadays, but what about the hidden idols we secretly carve for ourselves? For the person who is so determined never to be late that there are constant crises and everyone's life is a misery, for them time-keeping becomes an idol. Some people make an idol out of house-work, slaving night and day to prevent even a speck of dust settling!

The key to understanding self-indulgence and its effects is not to have a negative attitude and say, 'Oh well, that's just me, I'm like that!' Instead we must be open to the Holy Spirit, who not only sheds light on our sinfulness but, more important, on its causes too. The person who is jealous because ... bad-tempered because ... Tomorrow we will look at what happens when the Holy Spirit is allowed to work in us.

Prayer

> *Then they cried to the Lord in their need*
> *and he rescued them from their distress.*
> *He sent forth his word to heal them*
> *and saved their life from the grave.*
>
> *(Psalm 107 [106] : 19–20)*

The harvest of the Holy Spirit   *Lent 5/Friday*

> What the Spirit brings is very different: love, joy, peace, patience, kindness, goodness, trustfulness, gentleness and self-control ... Since the Spirit is our life, let us be directed by the Spirit.
>
> *(Galatians 5:22–23, 25)*

These are the harvest of the Holy Spirit, the signs that the Spirit is at work in our lives. If we were ever in danger of complacency, an examination of conscience against this particular list (even more so than yesterday's) would be sure to put an end to it at a stroke. It is in fact a more suitable test for a critical examination of ourselves than the previous one: am I always joyful, am I really peaceful, patient, good? Am I always trustful, gentle, and in complete control of myself?

Here is the test of Christian authenticity. We can preach beautiful sermons, sit on important committees, rush around helping people, quote scripture, hold prayer groups and Bible-study classes, and evangelize the whole world, but none of our efforts will have that stamp of authenticity if we do not reflect these precious fruits of the Spirit in our lives. There was once a line in a popular song that went, 'What the world needs now is love, sweet love; it's the only thing there's just too little of'. With today's catalogue in front of us I think we could come to the same conclusion about each one: what our world desperately needs and has too little of is love, joy, peace, patience, kindness, goodness, trustfulness, gentleness and self-control.

It is these manifestations of the Holy Spirit in believers which speak volumes to the sad, insecure and lost people in our society. They (perhaps without knowing it) are extremely sensitive to the Spirit communicating through these signs. They might not be able to explain it, but the Father draws them through the witness of Christians who radiate the Spirit in their lives.

I have seen the fruits of the Spirit bring unity among Christians in a way that human effort alone could never have achieved. If the Spirit is at work in people, they *are* one (sometimes to their own amazement). After some experience in the ecumenical field I can say that I have watched rigid barriers of prejudice melt away in people, in a way they can hardly credit themselves. If, while remaining true to our own traditions, we can view those of others with love, peace, patience, and so on, we will not be blocking the work of the Holy Spirit. Those who shout loudly, demonstrate and cause disturbances in the name of Christianity are manifestly far more attached to the list on the previous page than the one above...

The first word on the list, let us note, is love and I think in this context Paul has placed it first because all the others stem from it. Love is the first word in Christian growth and the last: it is the only thing that endures. Today let us read and reflect on chapter 13 of St Paul's first letter to the Corinthians in preparation for tomorrow.

Prayer

> *O God, be gracious and bless us*
> *and let your face shed its light upon us.*
> *So will your ways be known upon earth*
> *and all nations learn your saving help.*

(Psalm 67 [66] : 1–2)

Love   *Lent 5 / Saturday*

My dear people, let us love one another since love comes from God, and everyone who loves is begotten by God and knows God. Anyone who fails to love can never have known God, because God is love.

God's love for us was revealed when God sent into the world his only Son ... to be the sacrifice that takes our sins away. My dear people, since God has loved us so much, we too should love one another ... God will live in us and his love will be complete in us. We can know that we are living in him and he is living in us, because he lets us share his Spirit.

(1 John 4:7–13)

Herein lies the whole Christian message in one short passage. First it explains the Trinity: *God* is love, he loves us and sends his *Son* to give us life, and shares his *Spirit* with us. Second, it explains how we should respond. We too must love, love one another. Love is the beginning of the Christian vocation and the end: each precious life that exists is a reflection of God's love, each one unique and a beloved precious gem.

We now live in a world where the word 'love' can be about as meaningful as coca-cola. We throw the word to the winds like a bunch of confetti, which glitters for the moment then falls to the ground without significance. Love is in pop songs, TV commercials, written on T-shirts; love promotes, sells, packages. You don't need to be a psychologist to detect that when a person keeps going on about something it's usually because they have a problem, and maybe the modern obsession with the word love is a cry for help? And if the world is crying out for love, what it's really crying out for is God, because God is love.

For years I myself have struggled with God's commandment to love others: how could God, I wondered, make such impossible demands? Loving involves such a huge amount of human effort with no apparent returns for the trouble! Scripture readings and sermons on love were quite outside my range of experience: yes, I was aware of God's love for me and I believed I loved him—but his creatures were another matter altogether.

It is an agonizing situation, and not surprisingly, for we were created in love for love and to be living outside love is to be not really living at all. The truth is almost too simple to grasp: '*Anyone who fails to love can never have known God*'. It is these words that should be flashed across our TV screens several times a day, because in them lies the real meaning of the word. To know God is to know love, to be touched in that aching void within, to cry out with the blind man in the gospel, 'I only know that I was blind and *now* I can see!' (John 9:25).

How do we *know* God? By knowing Jesus, by immersing ourselves in his teaching, in prayer, in scripture, by accepting the gift of God's Spirit (whom he shares with us), who 'enlightens the eyes of our minds' as it says in Ephesians (1:18). The Holy Spirit will teach us to love others, since humanity left to itself does not truly have the capacity to give of itself (and true love is the emptying of self). Paul pointed out to the Philippians: 'It is God, for his own loving purpose, who puts both the will and the action into you' (2:13). If we allow God to put both of these in us, loving will never be a problem.

Prayer

> *O God, you are my God, for you I long;*
> *for you my soul is thirsting.*
> *My body pines for you*
> *like a dry, weary land without water.*
> *So I gaze on you in the sanctuary*
> *to see your strength and your glory.*
>
> *(Psalm 63 [62] : 1–2)*

Holy Week

Palm Sunday *Passion (Palm) Sunday*

Rejoice heart and soul, daughter of Zion!
Shout with gladness, daughter of Jerusalem!
See now, your king comes to you;
he is victorious, he is triumphant,
humble and riding on a donkey,
on a colt, the foal of a donkey.
He will banish chariots from Ephraim
and horses from Jerusalem;
the bow of war will be banished.
He will proclaim peace for the nations.
His empire shall stretch from sea to sea,
from the River to the ends of the earth.

(Zechariah 9:9–10)

When Jesus entered the city of Jerusalem on what we commemorate as Palm Sunday, his entry was in fulfilment of this prophecy of Zechariah. According to John's account (12:16), even the disciples did not realize this at the time, but it was only 'after Jesus had been glorified, they remembered that this had been written about him and that this was in fact how they had received him'.

The paradox in these events (and in the events of the whole Passion) is something we need to reflect on. 'He is victorious, he is triumphant, humble and riding on a donkey.' In human terms this is a complete contradiction:

how can one imagine a king arriving triumphantly and at the same time humbly riding on a donkey? If we compare what happens at any of our royal occasions—weddings or coronations—what we see above all is the splendour and opulence. But there is also something else: every branch of the police force, royal guards, cavalry is paraded; guns salute and planes fly past. Behind the crimson carpets and flashing jewels there is a massive show of strength, military and otherwise. We are triumphant and victorious, and here's how.

Since time began nations have been advertising their military strength, and the Bible itself is one long history of nations fighting nations. Yet the prophet Zechariah, five hundred years before the birth of Jesus, proclaimed that the Messiah would come not with a show of strength, but to 'banish horses and chariots' and 'proclaim peace for the nations'. His triumph would not be from human strength but in humility, and in such humiliating circumstances that his own people Israel would reject him. (Apart from that, Zechariah's message goes far beyond Holy Week—even to the end of time—when all nations will be at peace 'from sea to sea': through this humble event in the very centre of history God will eventually triumph totally.)

So what we see today is a quiet pilgrim entering the Holy City, surrounded by a small band of followers. Many of those there had seen Jesus raise Lazarus from the dead the previous day and knew he was 'special' in some way. So they waved their palm branches and laid down their cloaks and cried hosanna in welcome. I wonder if Jesus knew, as he looked at their demonstration of support and loyalty, that soon, when the going got rough, they would turn and run?

Our response today is to pray, not for human strength, but for the strength that comes from God; that through his strength we can learn to love him even when the going's rough; that we won't be simply Palm Sunday Christians, seeking all the comfortable aspects of religion. Instead let us recognize that, like the followers of Jesus, we too are surrounded by the enemy and that human weapons will not suffice, and learn how to follow Jesus, imitating his humble submission to the Father in all the circumstances of our lives. Above all, let us learn to recognize Jesus not only in praise and worship, but also in the midst of our difficulties, sorrows or frustrations: so many times in such situations we tend to close the door on him, forgetting that the resurrection happened in the midst of chaos and confusion. Let us pray for the grace to allow the man of sorrows to enter into and share all our sorrows. See now your king comes to you. *He* is triumphant, *he* is victorious ...

Prayer
> *I am sure now that the Lord*
> *will give victory to his anointed,*
> *will reply from his holy heaven*
> *with the mighty victory of his hand.*
> *(Psalm 20 [19] : 6)*

Judas   *Monday*

He was still speaking when Judas, one of the Twelve, appeared, and with him a large number of men armed with swords and clubs, sent by the chief priests and elders of the people. Now the traitor had arranged a sign with them. 'The one I kiss,' he had said 'he is the man. Take him in charge.' So he went straight up to Jesus and said, 'Greetings, Rabbi,' and kissed him. Jesus said to him, 'My friend, do what you are here for.'
(Matthew 26:47–50)

In reflecting on the events of Holy Week and on some of the principal characters involved, I think what we need to do is look at three distinct aspects: (*a*) how the person himself might have felt, (*b*) how Jesus felt, and (*c*) what is our own response. For me the simplest way to begin to reflect on these significant events—which mark the turning point in our entire history—is to look at them from the human level. I have long felt that nothing makes the gospels more alive and vivid than the essentially human nature of the story.

Jesus after all was 'a man like us in all things except sin,' feeling all the things we feel, sensitive to the same joys and sorrows. When the disciples came back from their first mission he was filled with spontaneous joy. He was a man who liked to hold little children close to him. Far from being the narrow killjoy some of his later followers would have us believe, it was thanks to him that the wine flowed freely at Cana; and seeing how the Pharisees labelled him a glutton and a boozer, we can be sure he enjoyed good food and drink!

What we need to try to recapture today is something of the extreme sorrow he experienced through the betrayal by a friend. Judas was not just a close friend of Jesus, he was an especially trusted friend. He had charge of the money, which is always a position of trust. (John is particularly scathing about Judas in his gospel and as he seems to have been the most sensitive of the disciples, I imagine it was a shattering blow to *his* trust of Judas too.)

John also intimates that Jesus was expecting to be betrayed: 'he was troubled in spirit' (13:21). Even so, what anguish he must have felt at the sight of this trusted friend approaching him in the garden! It is a betrayal and pain which human beings can identify with—often so great that many people are never able to give themselves completely in friendship, because of the devastating effects of possible rejection. In this respect Jesus was totally vulnerable.

Judas was tempted, and the moment he gave his consent to the temptation we read 'Satan entered him' (John 13:27). He left the disciples, went out, and John gives us symbolically the short sentence: 'Night had fallen'. Having consented to turn away from the light of the world, Judas entered into complete darkness. What was it that eventually changed his mind, that filled him with remorse and drove him to suicide? My own theory is that, after the kiss, when

Judas stood back expecting perhaps chastisement, accusation and anger, what he actually saw in the face of Jesus was an utter lack of condemnation. Instead there was total love and the words 'My friend...' This disarming situation, I believe, evoked two reactions. First, this could only be God—if he hadn't been sure before, he knew now. Then secondly, the guilt, the burden of which made him unable to cope with the consequences of his horrific mistake.

The sin of Judas was not the doubting, not the betrayal even, but his complete failure to understand God's forgiveness—unlike Peter who also betrayed, but was able to face his weakness and receive forgiveness. So our response must always be to seek to accept the forgiveness of God. People who turn their back on him and enter the darkness of sin have only to turn round and face that look of love. Let's remember this in our everyday lives, and learn to let go of pride, acknowledging our own acts of betrayal as part of our human weakness. Let us pray that we never commit the most destructive sin of all—to refuse God's forgiveness.

Prayer

> *If this had been done by an enemy*
> *I could bear his taunts.*
> *If a rival had risen against me,*
> *I could hide from him.*
>
> *But it is you, my own companion,*
> *my intimate friend!*
> *(How close was the friendship between us)*
> *We walked together in harmony*
> *in the house of God.*
> *(Psalm 55 [54] : 12–14)*

Mary the Mother of Jesus   *Tuesday*

As for Mary, she treasured all these things and pondered them in her heart.

(Luke 2:19)

Near the cross of Jesus stood his mother... Seeing his mother and the disciple he loved standing near her, Jesus said to his mother, 'Woman, this is your son'. Then to the disciple he said, 'This is your mother'. And from that moment the disciple made a place for her in his home.

(John 19:25–27)

Once again for me it is only at the ordinary human level that the role of Mary, throughout her life and in the events of Holy Week, can be properly grasped. If we go back to the beginning of Luke's gospel and read his account of the Annunciation and Mary's subsequent visit to her cousin Elizabeth, the picture we form in our minds is first of all of someone who has a firm belief. She must have been firmly rooted in the faith of Israel and have had a relationship with God. When she was greeted by the angel as being 'highly favoured' her response was not impulsive, not an instant and unthinking 'Yes'. At first she's thoughtful and asks herself what it all means; when the angel explains, she is so puzzled she asks another question: 'How can this come about, since I am a virgin?'

This is the irony of faith. We seek understanding of God, we profess faith, we worship, we declare him almighty—yet in reality we can only think in human terms. When the angel came to Mary, and Zechariah before her, in both cases the reaction was, How can this be? Both believed that the God of Israel had worked wonders for their people—but can't we identify with both of them when neither can at first believe his miracles could happen to them personally?

The angel explains to Mary that her cousin Elizabeth,

who everyone said was barren, is now in her sixth month of pregnancy, and says that nothing is impossible to God. Mary must have recalled that event in history when an angel said a similar thing to another barren woman, Abraham's wife Sarah—and now her response is 'Yes'. Although she doesn't understand she immediately yields with total trust, saying 'Let what you have said be done to me.'

I have heard it said that when Mary set out to visit Elizabeth it was entirely from altruistic motives—thinking of others, etc. I read it differently I'm afraid: if I had been told by an angel that I was to be the mother of the Son of God and that my cousin had had a similar visit from an angel, like Mary I would have gone to Elizabeth as fast as my legs would carry me—desperately needing to share the experience and make sure I hadn't been dreaming. I believe that great prayer we call the Magnificat was the sudden and overwhelming certainty of truth. It also offers one of the great insights into Mary: most of these spontaneous prayers that poured forth were from *scripture*. Like us she would not have had the words to express her deepest feelings, but she knew her scripture and at that moment what came out were the familiar words of God that had formed her in her faith.

After the birth of Jesus, it is recorded that she kept these things and pondered them. For that reason—and because she knew her scripture and was by nature a thoughtful person—I think she may have been perhaps one of only two people beside Jesus who had some understanding of the events of Holy Week. The other was John, and here, just before the final moment, the three of them share this intimate exchange. She had been told a sword would pierce her heart: she had had thirty years to prepare for this moment, but how hard it must have been for a mother to witness such a thing!

It's my personal belief that both she and John somehow knew this was the moment of victory—but that made not one jot of difference to their agony. For me the most vivid picture of Mary's suffering is the face of the Virgin in Michelangelo's Pieta. With an expression like that no further words need be said.

Let us today pray for the grace to say 'Yes' to God like
Mary, and learn to say it even in the midst of sorrow and
suffering. 'Let what you have said be done to me.'

Prayer As for me, I trust in your merciful love.
Let my heart rejoice in your saving help:
Let me sing to the Lord for his goodness to me,
singing psalms to the name of the Lord,
the Most High.
(Psalm 13 [12] : 5)

Peter   *Wednesday*

'Simon, Simon! Satan, you must know, has got his wish
to sift you all like wheat; but I have prayed for you,
Simon, that your faith may not fail, and once you have
recovered, you in your turn must strengthen your
brothers.' 'Lord,' he answered 'I would be ready to go
to prison with you, and to death.' Jesus replied, 'I tell
you, Peter, by the time the cock crows today you will
have denied three times that you know me'.

(Luke 22:31—34)

They seized him then and led him away, and they took
him to the high priest's house. Peter followed at a
distance. They had lit a fire in the middle of the
courtyard and Peter sat down among them, and as he
was sitting there by the blaze a servant-girl saw him,
peered at him, and said, 'This person was with him too'.
But he denied it. 'Woman,' he said 'I do not know him.'
Shortly afterwards someone else saw him and said,
' You are another of them'. But Peter replied, 'I am not,
my friend'. About an hour later another man insisted,

saying, 'This fellow was certainly with him. Why, he is a Galilean.' 'My friend,' said Peter 'I do not know what you are talking about.' At that instant, while he was still speaking, the cock crew, and the Lord turned and looked straight at Peter, and Peter remembered what the Lord had said to him, 'Before the cock crows today, you will have disowned me three times'. And he went outside and wept bitterly.

(Luke 22:54–62)

St Paul has said that the greatest virtues are faith, hope and love. And if I could sum up St Peter in one word, it would be 'hope'. More than any other of the gospel personalities it is he who provides us with an infinite source of hope in our journey of faith.

All through the gospel accounts Peter is continually putting his foot in it—and publicly at that! He has a most beautiful gift of spontaneous generosity, but his impulsiveness constantly lands him in trouble. His reaction to Jesus walking on the waves is 'I want to do it too', but he hasn't yet learnt how to keep his eyes fixed on Jesus: he acts in his own strength and fails in full view of everyone. But oh, he's so much more lovable than those who play it safe and sit tight!

All the time Peter is being drawn closer and closer to Jesus and we are aware of his love as it blossoms. He doesn't (we imagine) understand the teaching on the eucharist in John 6, but he still professes faith in Jesus: 'You have the message of eternal life, and we believe; we know that you are the Holy One of God' (6:68–69). Peter is not someone who insists on understanding every detail before committing himself: he believes that Jesus is the Messiah and is perfectly happy to follow him and learn on the way. He is deeply generous but has to learn how to channel this gift in the right direction; he was destined to be very great and he receives his training through his continued and repeated mistakes.

If only *we* could understand that this is the only pattern for real growth for those who wish to follow the call to discipleship. It's in our mistakes and failures that we learn to be humble, and only in our utter humility that we begin to grow strong.

For me one of the most poignant moments between the two of them was when Jesus told the disciples he would have to suffer and die. Peter takes Jesus aside and says, 'Heaven forbid! this can't happen to *you*, Lord' (Matthew 16:22). I believe that Jesus, knowing Satan will tempt him in any way he can to stop this happening, cries out to Peter, 'Get behind me, Satan' not in anger but in deep pain. How many of us find that when we are feeling really deep sorrow, we simply can't at that moment cope emotionally with the kind words and love of others?

Peter loved the Lord, as we all love him, and assumed that his love would endure anything. But his love was based on his own strength. He kept wanting to do things—build tents on top of the mountain of the transfiguration, draw a sword and fight off the soldiers at the arrest. But all the time Jesus is saying, 'No, it's not like that!' Again Peter gets it wrong when Jesus comes to wash his feet. 'Never' he cries, 'Not mine!' And again Jesus rebukes him: 'You'll have nothing in common with me if you don't let me do this'. (Anyone who follows Jesus *must* learn to serve others.) Peter replies impulsively, 'All right, wash all of me.' In other words, 'Whatever you say, Lord'.

When, in Luke's account, Peter claims to be ready to go to prison with him, even to die, I'm sure he really meant it. But he didn't understand what it would be like once the pressure was really on. He wanted to be brave: he didn't run away, he even tried to stay near Jesus. But as we know, he failed, the cock crew and Luke tells us that '*the Lord turned and looked straight at Peter*'. I think at that moment what Peter saw was a look of total compassion, of absolute love and forgiveness, that said, 'Now, Peter, that you finally understand human weakness, you can feed my sheep and lead my church, because you yourself will be able to identify and understand the sins and weaknesses of others'. Then he went outside and wept bitterly.

And it was this Peter who wept bitterly and reached the

very end of himself at the moment the cock crew, who stood up at the day of Pentecost and preached with such power that 3,000 were converted. He *did* go to prison; he did suffer the same tragic death as his Lord, but only after he had learned the lesson of utter human poverty. As we reflect on the role of Peter and on our own spiritual poverty, let's remember that every failure is an opportunity for growth, and the words of Jesus to Peter apply just as much to us: 'But I have prayed for you, that your faith may not fail'. Judas, unable to face himself, renounced his faith. Peter accepted his weakness, repented and became the Rock. 'You are Peter and on this rock I will build my Church. And the gates of the underworld can never hold out against it' (Matthew 16:18).

Prayer
> *I love you, Lord, my strength,*
> *my rock, my fortress, my saviour.*
> *My God is the rock where I take refuge;*
> *my shield, my mighty help, my stronghold.*
> *the Lord is worthy of all praise.*
> (Psalm 18 [19] : 2–3)

Gethsemane   *Holy (Maundy) Thursday*

They came to a small estate called Gethsemane, and Jesus said to his disciples, 'Stay here while I pray'. Then he took Peter and James and John with him. And a sudden fear came over him, and great distress. And he said to them, 'My soul is sorrowful to the point of death. Wait here and keep awake.' And going on a little further he threw himself on the ground and prayed that, if it were possible, this hour might pass him by. 'Abba (Father)!' he said 'Everything is possible for you. Take this cup away from me. But let it be as you, not I, would have it.' He came back and found them sleeping, and he said to Peter, 'Simon, are you asleep? Had you not the strength to keep awake one hour? You should be awake, and praying not to be put to the test. The spirit is willing, but the flesh is weak.' Again he went away and prayed, saying the same words. And once more he came back and found them sleeping, their eyes were so heavy; and they could find no answer for him. He came back a third time and said to them, 'You can sleep on now and take your rest. It is all over. The hour has come. Now the Son of Man is to be betrayed into the hands of sinners. Get up! Let us go! My betrayer is close at hand already.'

(Mark 14:32–42)

This reading (and its equivalent in Matthew 26) marks a significant turning-point in my own particular growth in faith. When I first read it in a prayerful way, it affected me so deeply as to change my whole attitude to faith. Although my over-crowded life had included time for *some* church activities, prayer, and so on, what I had totally missed out on was any knowledge of Jesus the person, the man 'like us in all things except sin'. It is strange how we can go through our lives practising our faith yet (as Isaiah put it so lucidly) 'we see but don't perceive, we hear but don't understand'.

What I suddenly understood from this reading was that Jesus was truly a man as well as truly God. Certainly I had always been taught this, but I hadn't grasped it or that our own human condition is so vividly reflected in his humanity.

The British are supposed to promote the stiff upper lip as a national virtue: to show emotion is to display weakness. We know how to face up to a crisis or, to use a modern idiom, keep our cool. Very few people, I believe, naturally live up to these standards and many suffer dreadfully from the effects of trying to keep a veneer of outer calm to disguise an inner turmoil. The message in the garden of Gethsemane from the Lord of lords who humbled himself to become like us is this:

don't be afraid to be afraid. It is part of our human condition, a part that cannot be hidden and overcome by human effort alone. We have to be like Jesus and come to terms with our fears; otherwise if we deny them, they manifest themselves in other ways, in depression or disease for instance.

Let us see how Jesus deals with this sudden fear that came over him, a distress so great it felt like the point of death. He doesn't say, 'Don't worry, I'll be OK'. He doesn't have a couple of stiff drinks or swallow a few tranquillizers. Instead, finding himself not quite able to cope, Jesus throws himself on the ground and cries, 'Abba (Father)!'—and in this action there is a lesson for the rest of humanity. When we are pressured, crushed, full of stress, bereaved or abandoned, we must learn how to throw ourselves on the ground and cry, 'Father! This is too much for me, I can't cope'.

Jesus did not want to accept death on the cross, but prays for strength to say, 'Yes'. 'Let it be as you, not I, would have it.' And it is interesting to note that he has to pray three times, saying the same thing over, before he is able to accept. 'The spirit is willing, but the flesh is weak.' Finding Peter asleep, Jesus is abandoned, with no one to offer comfort or companionship. We too seek comfort by surrounding ourselves with people, who may satisfy us temporarily yet prevent us from understanding our need for God. They cannot ultimately support our needs because they are beset with weaknesses just like us. In this situation, facing death alone, all Jesus can do is keep crying 'Father!', and finally Jesus *is* given the strength to accept the will of God. The hour has come, the decision is made.

For me one personal reflection is that Gethsemane teaches us how totally unacceptable death is. We were created for life and not for death. How grieved God must be that though his Son Jesus has overcome death on the cross, yet so many people do not choose life through him but instead shrug their shoulders, prepared to accept death with all its horror and finality. Let us pray today that the world

will learn the lessons of Gethsemane and understand that
human strength is not enough to face the enemy. Let us pray
that *we* stay awake to perceive and understand, and that the
whole of humanity will eventually learn to cry out, 'Abba,
Father!'

Prayer

Have mercy on me, God, have mercy
for in you my soul has taken refuge.
In the shadow of your wings I take refuge
till the storms of destruction pass by.

I call to God the Most High,
to God who has always been my help.
(Psalm 57 [56] : 1–2)

Good Friday *Good Friday*

Without beauty, without majesty (we saw him),
no looks to attract our eyes;
a thing despised and rejected by men,
a man of sorrows and familiar with suffering,
a man to make people screen their faces;
he was despised and we took no account of him.
And yet ours were the sufferings he bore,
ours the sorrows he carried.
But we, we thought of him as someone punished,
struck by God, and brought low.
Yet he was pierced through for our faults,
crushed for our sins.
On him lies a punishment that brings us peace,
and through his wounds we are healed . . .

Hence I will grant whole hordes for his tribute,
he shall divide the spoil with the mighty,

for surrendering himself to death
and letting himself be taken for a sinner,
while he was bearing the faults of many
and praying all the time for sinners.

(Isaiah 53:2–5, 12)

Today is a day to be quiet and spend time reflecting on the Passion narratives. I would recommend reading either John chapters 18 and 19 or Matthew chapters 26 and 27; and in addition the *whole* of the above text (which is actually vv. 13–15 of ch. 52 and all of ch. 53). For Christians this passage from Isaiah, the Song of the Suffering Servant, written approximately 600 years before Jesus lived, sounds uncannily like an eye-witness account of the events of Good Friday. It is a beautiful and deeply sensitive piece of writing, and if we meditate quietly on each verse it will provide us with a vivid picture of the sufferings of Jesus and his destiny as Saviour of the world. I personally feel it is a mistake to 'screen our faces' from the suffering servant. It is only when we are sensitive to the sorrow and suffering of the Passion that we can begin to comprehend the joy and victory of the cross. The idea of screening our faces is akin to the psalmist's warning not to harden our hearts (see Lent 3)—in either case our senses are dulled so as never to experience true heartfelt joy.

Good Friday should not be a day just for mourning or even feeling guilt: it should be a day of reaction and response, a day to ask ourselves a question—How am I going to respond to what God is saying? Am I going to react to the cry of Jesus on the cross, 'I thirst'? God thirsts for his people, thirsts to be with them. All through our scripture meditations during Lent we have heard the same message: 'Come back, seek me, hear me, learn from me.'

Today we must, like Mary, decide to say 'Yes'. If we are nominal Christians we must become committed; if we are committed Christians we must become disciples; and if we are disciples we must become saints. We must (as Paul says) 'shine like bright stars', and give light to this darkened, confused and insecure world (Philippians 2:15). And if we feel unworthy let us throw ourselves down at the foot of the cross, with all our sinfulness and weaknesses. It doesn't matter if we're failures, burdened with guilt, unable to cope; whatever our problems and sorrows we must turn to the source of life and say 'Yes'. For 'on him lies a punishment that brings us peace, and through his wounds we are healed'.

Prayer

> *Blessed be the God and Father of our Lord Jesus Christ, a gentle Father and a God of all consolation who comforts us in all our sorrows, so that we can offer others in their sorrows the consolation we have received from God ourselves. Indeed, as the sufferings of Christ overflow to us so does our consolation overflow. Blessed be God.*

Joseph of Arimathaea   *Holy Saturday*

Then a member of the council arrived, an upright and virtuous man named Joseph. He had not consented to what the others had planned and carried out. He came from Arimathaea, a Jewish town, and he lived in the hope of seeing the kingdom of God. This man went to Pilate and asked for the body of Jesus. He then took it down, wrapped it in a shroud and put him in a tomb which was hewn in stone in which no one had yet been laid. It was Preparation Day and the Sabbath was imminent. Meanwhile the women who had come from Galilee with Jesus were following behind. They took note of the tomb and of the position of the body. Then they returned and prepared spices and ointments.

(Luke 23:50–56)

Here is a character from the gospels about whom we know very little, except that all four gospels record his role in the burial of Jesus. Yet for me his action symbolizes something very significant: Joseph is a lesson to all of us in *doing what we can*, in offering what we have.

Sometimes we can become over-zealous—perhaps for reasons of pride. We can want to do great things for God— we have often read about born-again Christians wanting to give up everything and preach the gospel. But sometimes we have to be content to give the Lord what we have, and love him and serve him *where we are*. It's like the legend on a card I once saw: written under the picture of a small flower was simply 'Bloom where you are planted'.

But to get back to Joseph. He had obviously believed that Jesus was the Messiah (in John's account we read that he was a secret disciple of Jesus; see 19:38). He was an important member of the Sanhedrin, and had not consented to their evil plan. How frustrated he must have been, along with Nicodemus, the other member of the council who believed in Jesus (19:39). They must have tried to prevent the crucifixion and felt such anguish at what must have seemed like total failure. Yet we read that Joseph 'lived in hope of seeing the kingdom of God'! There is a moral for us all here when things look bleak, when we think everything's going in the wrong direction, when we feel we haven't been able to achieve what we wanted to achieve. We simply live quietly in hope of seeing God's kingdom! Like Joseph we do what we can. He couldn't prevent Jesus' death, so he offered two things: a tomb and a shroud to wrap the body in—little knowing that what he was offering was actually going to bear witness to the resurrection, not only for the disciples but for the rest of time.

In the synoptic gospel accounts Mary Magdalene and the other Mary watched the burial: they saw the stone and knew that soldiers were guarding it—and it was their witness that first brought the news of the resurrection!

We can compare the story of Joseph with several others that occur in the gospels. For instance, with the small boy who donated two small fishes and five barley loaves (John 6:9). What an insignificant and seemingly paltry offering when 5,000 people needed food! Yet a small gift given to Jesus is transformed into something so powerful and far-reaching that it is quite beyond the conception of the giver. And there were others who gave what they had: the woman with the alabaster jar of expensive perfumed oil (Mark 14:3–9), and the widow with her mite (Mark 12:41–44). The lesson for us in all these characters is that what we really need to give is ourselves. Joseph of Arimathaea had experienced conversion, had given God his heart. What we must learn from him is that one small, unimportant life given to God can give to others more than we can ever dream of or imagine.

Prayer

> *Commit your life to the Lord,*
> *trust in him and he will act,*
> *so that your justice breaks forth like the light,*
> *your cause like the noon-day sun.*
>
> *Be still before the Lord and wait in patience.*
> (Psalm 37 [36] : 5–6)

Behold the Lamb of God   *Easter Sunday*

Meanwhile Mary stayed outside near the tomb, weeping. Then, still weeping, she stooped to look inside, and saw two angels in white sitting where the body of Jesus had been, one at the head, the other at the feet. They said, 'Woman, why are you weeping?' 'They have taken my Lord away' she replied 'and I don't know where they have put him'. As she said this she turned round and saw Jesus standing there, though she did not recognize him. Jesus said, 'Woman, why are you weeping? Who are you looking for?' Supposing him to be the gardener, she said, 'Sir, if you have taken him away, tell me where you have put him, and I will go and remove him'. Jesus said, 'Mary!' She knew him then and said to him in Hebrew, 'Rabbuni!'—which means Master. Jesus said to her, 'Do not cling to me, because I have not yet ascended to the Father. But go and find the brothers, and tell them: I am ascending to my Father and your Father, to my God and your God.' So Mary of Magdala went and told the disciples that she had seen the Lord and that he had said these things to her.

(John 20:11–18)

This account of Mary Magdalene's early visit to the tomb symbolizes, for me, the point of total sanctity in the life of a human being. She illustrates that complete surrender to God that one associates with saints. Earlier in her life she had been the woman from whom Jesus cast out seven demons (Luke 8:2). What a state of mind she must have been in! Was it her courage that initially drew her near to Jesus in order to be set free? Or maybe it wasn't courage, perhaps she didn't even expect that her life would be totally transformed; perhaps she just had an urge to see him, to be near to him, like a moth in the dark night mysteriously and irresistibly drawn in to the light. Perhaps too she never

121

expected the eyes of incarnate love to turn in *her* direction. How could she, in such a wretched condition, expect such tender compassion and mercy?

In Mary Magdalene we see the explanation of the words of Jesus 'the man who is forgiven little, loves little' (Luke 7:47). When we become aware of our sinfulness and allow Jesus to set us free, I believe the first stage of loving is sheer *gratitude*. We are, as C. S. Lewis said, 'surprised by joy'.

Mary's love was not a fair-weather kind of love. She is prepared to go all the way: she is present at the crucifixion, she doesn't run away from suffering but witnesses and shares every painful moment. Afterwards it seems that nothing can separate her from her beloved Lord—she follows him even in death, watching as he's laid in the tomb. When she returns, even his body has gone and she experiences the dark desolation of someone who can't find God in the midst of a tragic situation. It is right here that we encounter the stuff of which saints are made. The disciples have seen the empty tomb and gone home (v. 10), but not Mary—she stays, she weeps, she searches, she does not give up in the face of total disaster. 'Tell me where you have put him, and I will go . . . ' This persistent and uncompromising love is requited with one word—'Mary!' This is the moment of recognition, a moment unparalleled in the history of creation when 'a light shines in the dark, a light that darkness *could not overpower*' (John 1:5) and Mary Magdalene is the first person in history to see the risen Lord: Mary the convert, the sinner who had been set free, the lover whose love remained undiminished in the midst of confusion and disaster.

Today, as we go forward to live our lives in the full light of the Resurrection, let us remember that the risen Jesus calls each one of us individually, *by name*. Let us pray that we will each of us recognize him when he speaks our name, and respond like Mary with the greatest gift of all, the gift of love.

Prayer

> *On my bed, at night, I sought him*
> *whom my heart loves.*
> *I sought but did not find him.*
> *So I will rise and go through the City;*
> *in the streets and squares*
> *I will seek him whom my heart loves.*
> *... I sought but did not find him.*
> *The watchmen came upon me*
> *on their rounds in the City:*
> *'Have you seen him whom my heart loves?'*
>
> *Scarcely had I passed them*
> *than I found him whom my heart loves.*
> *I held him fast, nor would I let him go.*

(Song of Songs 3:1–4)

More titles from the Bible Reading Fellowship:

A Feast for Advent

Delia Smith

'Delia Smith's journey through Advent touches the
season beautifully. It is hopeful, full of love and trust,
and encouraging to all those who wish, like her, to
break the bread of God's Word and to share it with
others.' *David Konstant, Bishop of Leeds.*

'I suspect that, if we're honest, most of us come into
the "don't know" category where Advent is
concerned.

'Delia Smith has ensured that from now on things
will be different. It goes without saying that in her case
the puddings and pies will be superlatively well
attended to; but in this little book, with all the
simplicity which is her hallmark, she points to the deep
underlying significance of the weeks leading up to
Christmas.

'Delia provides us with the brief daily meditations
and reflections which will sharpen our appetite and
longing for the events of Christmas, but which also
provide a satisfaction all their own.

'Delia Smith has made it possible for us to experience the real joy of Christmas.' *Mary Craig, writer and
broadcaster.*

ISBN 0 7459 2330 5

O Come, O Come Emmanuel
A First Guide to Using Scripture in Groups

Bill Redmond and Paul Murray

O Come, O Come Emmanuel consists of four scripture studies which come complete with leader's notes, additional background information, participants' worksheets (which may be photocopied) and suggested prayer material. The book includes full training notes on how to use the scripture studies. Also here are detailed guidelines on how to develop further Bible studies based on the same method.

Intended primarily for use during Advent, *O Come, O Come Emmanuel* may be used with a variety of groups. Anybody could lead a group using this material as no previous experience in leading scripture groups is presumed by the authors. The book will introduce many to the joys of shared scripture study and will also be welcomed by experienced group leaders who are looking for fresh ideas and approaches.

Available from bookshops £4.25 (UK), or direct from BRF (single copy, including postage & packing) £5.00 (UK).

ISBN 0 7459 2328 3

New Daylight
A pattern for daily Bible reading

Edited by Shelagh Brown

Each day's reading contains a Bible passage (printed out in full, from the version chosen by the contributor), along with a brief commentary and explanation, and a suggestion for prayer, meditation or reflection.

The sections of comment often draw on and reflect the experiences of the contributors themselves and thus offer contemporary and personal insights into the readings.

Sunday readings focus on the themes of Prayer and Holy Communion.

New Daylight is published three times a year, in January, May and September.

New Daylight is also available in a large print version.

Individual subscriptions (direct from BRF) covering 3 issues for under 5 copies, payable in advance (including postage & packing) at £7.95 each p.a. (Large print £12.00 each p.a.)

Group subscriptions (direct from BRF) covering 3 issues for 5 copies or more, sent to one address (post free) at £6.45 each p.a. (Large print £10.50 each p.a.)

Copies may also be obtained from Christian bookshops at £2.15 each (Large print £3.50 per copy).

Guidelines to the Bible
Week by week Bible reading for thought,
prayer and action

Edited by Grace Emmerson and John Parr

Guidelines contains running commentary, with
introductions and background information, arranged
in weekly units. Each week's material is usually broken
up into at least six sections. Readers can take as much or
as little at a time as they wish. The whole 'week' can be
used at a sitting, or split up into convenient parts: this
flexible arrangement allows for one section to be used
each weekday. A Bible will be needed. The last section
of each week is usually called 'Guidelines' and has
points for thought, meditation and prayer. A short list
of books, to help with further reading, appears at the
end of some contributions.

   Guidelines is published three times a year, in
January, May and September.

Individual subscriptions (direct from BRF) covering 3 issues for
under 5 copies, payable in advance (including postage & packing) at
£7.95 each p.a.

Group subscriptions (direct from BRF) covering 3 issues for 5 copies
or more, sent to one address (post free) at £6.45 each p.a.

Copies may also be obtained from Christian bookshops at £2.15
each.

First Light

Bible activities for children

Edited by Jan Ainsworth

First Light notes set out to make Bible reading fun—but thoughtful fun.

The notes are designed to bring the Bible alive and involve readers with the help of quizzes, puzzles and activities all based on the *Alternative Service Book* Sunday readings.

First Light can be used at home, church or in Sunday School.

Notes for group leaders are available with each issue, with advice and suggestions on how to use *First Light*.

First Light notes are fully illustrated and are written by a team of contributors—Jan Ainsworth, Diane Webb, Sharon Swain and Judith Sadler.

First Light is published three times a year, in January, May and September.

Individual subscriptions (direct from BRF) covering 3 issues for under 5 copies, payable in advance (including postage & packing) at £7.95 each p.a.

Group subscriptions (direct from BRF) covering 3 issues for 5 copies or more, sent to one address (post free) at £6.45 each p.a.

Copies may also be obtained from Christian bookshops at £2.15 each.